FEB 99,

TO SIR STEWART

WITH MY VERY BEST REGARDS
AND GRATEFUL THANKS FOR YOUR
SUPPORT AND FRIENDSHIP

JOHN HILLBERY

Please See the acknowledgments

John

The Wizard

The Wizard of Is

Tom Thiss

Fairview Press   *Minneapolis*

Published by Fairview Press, 2450 Riverside Avenue South, Minneapolis, MN 55454.

Library of Congress Cataloging-in-Publication Data
Thiss, Thomas, 1929—
    The wizard of is / by Thomas Thiss
        p. cm.
    Includes bibliographical references.
    ISBN 0-925190-48-9
    1. Stress management. I. Title.
RA785.T475   1995   93-49693
155.9'042—dc20   CIP

Jacket design: Circus Design
Jacket photo: ViewPoint

First printing: May 1995
Printed in the United States of America

99 98 97 96 95   7 6 5 4 3 2 1

Publisher's note: Fairview Press publishes books and other materials related to the subjects of physical health, mental health, chemical dependency, and family issues. Its publications, including *The Wizard of Is*, do not necessarily reflect the philosophy of Fairview Hospital and Healthcare Services or their treatment programs.

For a current catalog of Fairview Press titles,
please call this toll-free number: 1-800-544-8207.

To George, my brother, who never saw this book.
But if he had, we all would be wiser
for his practical insights and
his great compassion.

We have what we seek. It is there all the time.
And if we give it time, it will make itself known to us.

—Thomas Merton

Contents

*The spirit must lean on science as its guide
in the world of reality,
and science must turn to the spirit
for the meaning of life.*

—Richard Wilhelm
*The Secret of the Golden Flower:
A Chinese Book of Life*

Preface

Search your heart and see. The way to do is to be.
—Lao-tzu

While living in London in the mid-1980s, I worked with an extraordinary visionary leader. He was an inexhaustible source of wisdom and inspiration. On one occasion while addressing a group of top-level managers, he said, "Don't be concerned about what you do. Pay attention first to what you are, and then bring those qualities into all that you do." That statement, exceedingly uncommon for a chief executive, struck me as profoundly wise. He was telling us to attend to our being. Today in America, we would say, "Get yourself together before you act." Although this book had many streams that gave rise to it, that one statement seemed to set its course.

I was repeatedly struck with my mentor's ability to move through a series of diverse encounters and approach each one focused and fully present. In a meeting he always took a few moments to center himself and to feel the energy in the setting before he began. He became the model for one of the main characters in this book, the Wizard of Is.

While living abroad, you often learn more about your own country than the one you are living in because you see America through the eyes of an expatriate. Often when entering the States after an extended time overseas, I would feel assaulted by the frenzied, stressful pace of life. It was as if everybody and everything were shouting at me. Soon, however, I would find myself swept up in the stream of events, a participant in the frenetic pace that had bothered me a short time before. It occurred to me that most people are not aware of this because they have not had sufficient exposure to anything different. They have accepted stressful lives not knowing they have other choices.

I knew that the global realignment process that was causing much dislocation in our country would continue, and the dizzying changes in our business marketplace would only accelerate. These changes we could do nothing about. The only stress-reducing option available to us, other than burning out or dropping out, seemed to be drawing on our deeper inner resources. Somehow, if we could bring the best of us to the moment we would neither be victims nor exploiters, but rather people with choices. Making these choices would be more a matter of using our internal resources than being victims of external forces over which we had little control.

A "how-to-be book" appealed to me because all the focus in our culture was on doing . . . and it appeared to me we weren't doing very well! We are beings by nature, but we have become "doings" by choice. The quality of those choices is directly related to our being, to who and what we are. It seems as if we have things backwards. Development is an inside-out process. It takes work. There are no shortcuts. As such, we need to know more about ourselves, our values, our talents, and our purpose for being. These existential issues need to be addressed if our lives are to be truly authentic. Otherwise, we are living lies.

I have been in the training and development business for over thirty years. During that time, I have taught courses or consulted in thirty-nine countries on six continents. In the last few years, I have seen remarkable changes. Many of those changes, however, we have been advocating for twenty-five years, and most are not happening as fast as they could. They are happening, however, because now they are economic necessities. A business changes when its life is threatened.

The same is true with individuals. I am continually amazed at what it takes to get people to change their ways. I believe this is so because most people are not in charge of their lives. They have turned that responsibility over to other authorities—corporations, money lenders, governing and political bodies, churches, medical groups, associations, peer groups, parent educators, and so on. I hear it in statements like this: "I'd like to, but I've got two kids in college. . . ." or "I think you're right, but my boss. . . ." or "My doctor told me I had to. . . ." These authorities have huge vested interests in the status quo. The people representing these hugely influential interests make the big decisions for us, leaving us with only the cosmetic changes. The most important question we could ask ourselves is, "Who's in charge of me?" And if we are honest, most would not like to hear our own answers.

Most of us have abdicated our priceless right of choice; we are really not aware that we are no longer in charge of our own lives. We think we are calling the shots, but the big shots are calling the big shots! The loss of personal responsibility has been a gradual, erosive process. When made aware of this, however, the choice to set it right is ours. Nothing is more stressful than feeling that you no longer have control over your own life. This book is a fifteen-part process for recovering that lost or threatened feeling. For you this choice may be so daunting that you opt to continue your life the way it has been. Governed by fixed habits, mindsets, thought patterns, beliefs, and perceptions that decide for you, you then unknowingly await a personal crisis. Only trauma can bring about needed changes.

If we were really in charge of ourselves, change would be simple and quick. We would run the proposed change by our value system and determine if the change were consonant with our purpose. If so, we would go with it. If not, it's a nonstarter. To get to this point, however, we have a lot of work to do on ourselves. That's the inner journey the Wizard of Is talks about in this book. The journey starts either with curiosity or a crisis. For the vast majority, the latter does it for us. Life keeps giving us a wake-up call. The role of the Wizard in the book is to give readers a wake-up call, sounding the alarm of curiosity, not crisis.

The goal of traditional wisdom has always been to awaken to the truth. This truth is what each of us must seek for ourselves. One thing is certain: Truth comes from within, from the heart of our being. Discovering this truth is the most exciting journey ever undertaken, to a place where nobody has ever been before. The risk of not taking the inner journey is a life not truly lived. The reward of doing so is a life fulfilled. No risk, no reward. This book is a summons for all who wish to take the first steps to a less stressful and more exciting human beginning.

Acknowledgments

On the highest plain one does not act, one is.
—George Bernard Shaw

This book had its origins in London, England. While living there from 1983–89, I commuted to the United States several times a year where I spent many weekends between consulting assignments writing early versions of this book.

In London, A. H. Abedi and John Hillbery gave me inspiration for much of the conceptual underpinnings of the text. In the United States, my colleagues at Organizational Resources International, Bob Alberts and Bob Spiewak, have been my loyal friends and cofacilitators in many seminars where these ideas were tested and refined.

Pat Samples gave me early editorial help of great value and pointed me to Jay Johnson, my editor at Fairview Press who, more than anyone, has made this book a reality. Jay has been this book's most ardent champion and its most insightful critic. My thanks also to Ed Wedman at Fairview whose great encouragement and patience made it all happen, and to Mark Hinton and Julie Odland for their thoughtful editorial help.

Rick and Jody Avery, Ralph Copleman, Anna Currence, Jim Gaughan, Dick Leider, Harrison Owen, Norm Shealy, and Ruth Stricker all read various versions of the unedited manuscript and gave me needed support and criticism.

My family has watched this evolve over a longer time than any of us thought possible. My four boys—Eric, Ted, Peter, and Michael—were the subjects of many of my early management "experiments" at home. Through raising them, I learned more about management than from all the books I ever read. As young adults, they have been patient champions of this project, code named "The Wiz," as has my wife, Cokey.

The writings of several people had a strong influence on my thinking. Among them were Herbert Benson, Edward de Bono, Norman Cousins, Vaclav Havel, Hans Selye, and Carl Jung.

A special thanks to Chris Keeble for a great story, to Frank Beddor for his wonderful promotional help, to Joe Ehrenberg for his thoughtful and caring critique, and to my parents, Chuck and Alice, who are both in their nineties and living examples of good stress management.

Lastly, I owe a measure of thanks to two long-deceased basset hounds, Douglas and Alphie, whose great stress-reduction capabilities gave me inspiration for two of the chapters in this book.

Tom Thiss
March 1995

Introduction

The true perfection of man lies not in what man has,
but in what man is.
—Oscar Wilde

In a little town in middle America lived an unpretentious
man, a doer of largely uncelebrated deeds of personal
thoughtfulness. He lived simply and he lived alone. Yet he
was not, as you might expect, a lonely man. Children loved
him. He attracted them like a Pied Piper, delighting them with
tales and with the treasures he collected on his many travels.
Above all other traits, he had a warm and welcoming way.

Perhaps what endeared him most to the young people in
town was his message of how to be. He spoke hopefully and
confidently of a better world, as if it were actually so . . . and
he made a world that isn't always pleasant seem as if it were.
He spoke with an assuring certainty of a deeper reality that
lies behind what we see, the apparent, and he talked about the
reality of what *is*. This is why the town's children and their
parents called him the "Wizard of Is."

There was mystery around the Wizard. When you were
with him, you felt a sense of serenity that set you apart from
the frenzy and uncertainty of the world. This calmness caused
the grown-ups in town to wonder, "What does the Wizard
know that we don't?" In times of stress and change, it is com-
forting to be with a man who appears to have it all together.

Not much is known about his life, but rumors abound.
Some people thought he was a cult figure. Others just regard-

ed him as strange, and they kept a polite distance from him. The townspeople, by calling him the Wizard, sometimes conjured up questionable charges of mysticism and the supernatural against him. But these accusations were unproven, and the worst that could be said about the man is that he was different. This was precisely why children loved him and some grown-ups regarded him with suspicion. To many he symbolized a threat to their lifestyles—after all, how could someone be so calm and confident when the world continues to raise the bar of expectations for us?

The Wizard's prominence has grown in recent years. He has become a folk hero, a guru for searchers. This, too, has distressed some townspeople, as it has brought a stream of pilgrims into their small community and deepened their suspicion of strangers.

One day I was able to witness this remarkable man firsthand, for I reached a time in my life—caught up with stress and business concerns—when I felt compelled to visit the Wizard.

1
The Answers within

If you have come to me for answers,
then you have traveled in vain.

I **first** came to the Wizard when I was in my middle years. I was troubled and apprehensive, but eager to learn. The Wizard met me at the door, and he immediately offered me a cup of Tranquilitea, his favorite herbal tea blend. When I finished the tea, the Wizard asked me what I did for a living. I told him that I was a manager. With that, the Wizard smiled knowingly and asked, "Do you enjoy being a healer?"

Wondering if I had been misunderstood, I hesitated then replied uneasily, "A healer?"

"Why, yes," said the Wizard. He laid his hand gently on my shoulder. "Do you not know you are in a healing profession? There are a lot of people who do their jobs every day, but they are living fragmented lives. Anyone who helps them put the pieces together is a healer. Healing is the process of becoming more whole, less fragmented. The word *holy* comes from the same root word."

The Wizard stopped a moment, smiled at me again, then added with a nod, "I will wager you did not know you were in a holy profession!" With that we both laughed, and my initial tension dissolved.

"I never thought of managing as a healing profession, let alone holy," I said. "If anyone needs healing, it's probably me."

"That is precisely the point," affirmed the Wizard. "We cannot do much for others if we are not whole ourselves. Have you ever thought how much damage 'sick' or fragmented doctors can do to their patients?

"*Iatrogenic* is a word that describes illness caused by a doctor's inappropriate diagnosis, manner, or treatment. The word *iatros* is Greek for 'physician.' Iatrogenic illness is induced in a patient by a doctor's inept words and actions. It is very common, but probably no more common for doctors than for nurses, teachers, factory workers, parents, or any other profession. In business I call it 'managenic illness,' or problems people have that are induced by their managers."

"What kinds of problems?"

"Managenic problems are epidemic—low self-esteem, lack of confidence, dependency, guilt, anxiety, depression, fear, and anger, just to name a few. Stress, with all of its physical consequences, is the big problem. Managing a business or a family is a huge responsibility. First, we have a job to do on ourselves before we can be of help to others. In this sense, we are all managers—managers of ourselves. It is a full-time job." The Wizard looked at me for a reaction.

"I guess that's why I'm here." I squirmed a bit in my chair. "I need help, and I'm looking for some answers," I said in my most businesslike manner.

"Have you come to find a cure for stress, a cure for the hurting we all experience?" asked the Wizard.

I was a bit taken aback by his question. "Well, I'm not sure. I don't know if I need to be cured of anything."

"The word *cure* comes from the Latin *curare* meaning 'to take care of.' Let me put it another way. Are you looking for someone to take care of you?" the Wizard asked as he poured more tea into my cup.

"I'm quite capable of caring for myself," I said a bit defensively.

"Good," replied the Wizard, softening his directness with a shrug of the shoulders. "Being in a holy profession, you should know that in the priesthood, *cura animarum* literally means the 'care of souls' or 'pastoral care.' The priesthood of management is no different. Good managers care for their people, as good parents care for their children, but they also need care. Let me rephrase my question. Have you come to me for pastoral care?"

"I guess so. All I know is, I've got problems and I came to you for answers."

The Wizard reflected for a moment, and then spoke softly to me. He measured his words, as if to make each one count. "If you have come to me for answers, then you have traveled in vain. The answers you seek lie within you."

These words bothered me. I had heard similar advice before and I thought it was a cop-out. I had come for help and he seemed to be passing the buck. After all, if I had the answers, I wouldn't be here! Trying to mask my discomfort, I quipped, "If they do lie within, they haven't made themselves visible yet!"

He laughed and I did as well although mine was a little forced.

"I'm glad to see you laugh. Laughter is one of the best healers," said the Wizard. "I call it 'aerobics for the spirit.' Laughing helps us maintain our mental fitness. As for the answers that have not yet revealed themselves to you, do not worry. Answers take time and patience. They are reticent by nature. We have to prepare ourselves to receive them, even to recognize them. It is almost always when we are in a relaxed state that answers make themselves known to us, but they will come. Laughter helps prepare the way." I could tell the Wizard was pleased with my growing ease.

"Interesting that you should say that," I said, squinting my eyes and looking intently at my new mentor. "People always tell me I should try to relax more."

The Wizard shook his head. "Relax, yes. Try, no. Trying seldom helps you relax. That's like striving to sleep—it doesn't work. Relaxation is a natural, allowing process. Often we try too hard. Just allow yourself to relax. Your body knows how to do it, if you give it permission.

"The truth you seek to your everyday problems is really quite simple, but simple is seldom easy. An awareness of what lies within you is the key. When you tune into the inside, then the outside will take care of itself. Right now, you have access to all the power you need. Call it God, Spirit, or intuition, if you will, but when you discover your inner power, you will have your answers. That is what is, and that is how to be in life."

There was a knock at the door, and the Wizard introduced me to two neighbor boys. They brought him a fistful of feathers, some spoor, a maiden hair fern, and assorted artifacts that they had just found in the woods. They knew "Mister Wizard" would tell them all about their discoveries, and he did.

Suggestions

The Wizard had the following thoughts for me:

1. Lighten up. Don't take yourself too seriously.
2. Laugh more often. Norman Cousins, in his classic *Anatomy of an Illness,* documents the salutary effect laughter had in overcoming his illness. He watched old "Candid Camera" classics and Marx Brothers films. When his laughter became a problem for other hospital patients, he checked into a hotel room.
3. Practice looking for humor in daily situations. Comedians get their material from the grist of daily affairs. Look for the absurd and laugh about it.
4. Practice the art of play again. Eric Berne, founder of Transactional Analysis, said each of us has three ego states—the parent, the adult, and the child. All are essential for the whole personality, but the most important is the child. Berne said we should "let our child out to play" at least two hours every day. What two hours do you have in store for your child today?
5. Be more spontaneous. Life is a happening. Have fewer planned events and more happenings.
6. Celebrate more often. The public relations director of Pommery, a champagne producer in Rheims, France, does

not buy the idea that champagne is for special occasions. He said, "You don't wait for the event to happen to celebrate with champagne. You make it happen *with* champagne. Champagne *is* the event! (Champagne est la fête!)

2
Stress and the Demand for Change

It is not what happens to us that hurts us,
but rather how we take it.

In the days that followed my first meeting with the Wizard I stayed in town at a small residential hotel. It was a few days before I could see the Wizard again. I had difficulty sleeping, often pacing my room at night unable to quiet my thoughts. My mind was filled with conflicting thoughts and emotions. Meeting the Wizard was so different from my daily routine. It felt strange to me, yet at the same time, I was curiously attracted to this man and his message. I didn't know what to make of it all. What I did know, however, was that I was drawn to a certain ineffable quality in the Wizard, and I wanted to experience more of it.

The meeting with the Wizard had already revealed something startlingly simple to me. I was one of those fragmented people the Wizard spoke about, and I desperately longed for a sense of wholeness. I needed healing, though I had never thought of it that way. I also was troubled by the growing awareness that my ineffective words and actions had caused a lot of "managenic" problems for the people I supervised. Admittedly, I was stressed and I didn't have my act together, but I had always blamed it on the circumstances around me— my busy schedule, workload, responsibilities to my family.

In a few days it was clear to me why I had come to the Wizard. If I were to be a healer, I had some work to do on myself. It startled me that the people I managed looked to me for healing. I felt overwhelmed and remembered the Wizard saying, "The answers you seek lie within you." I needed to hear more—a lot more.

When we met again it was an early Spring day. The Wizard was behind his house removing his birch-bark canoe from winter storage.

"I've never seen a canoe like this except in Native American museums," I said. "Is this the way they used to make them?"

"It is completely authentic except for one compromise with modernity. I have used a polyurethane sealant to caulk the seams rather than spruce sap, bear grease, and charcoal as the Ojibway would have done. The early French Voyageurs who opened up this area to the fur trade in the eighteenth century used longer versions of this canoe for crossing the Great Lakes and navigating the larger rivers, but they had to recaulk their canoes every evening. I did not think that would be very practical."

"Why isn't it white like the bark of the paper birch? I asked.

"You are looking at the inner bark of the tree which is on the outside of the canoe. The inner bark is softer and more pliable and will take more bruising after it has soaked up some water. The white outer bark is impervious to water but is more likely to tear on rocks so that is on the inside. The Ojibway had another reason for doing so. They liked to decorate their canoes by etching designs on the darker bark. They crafted designs in relief by scraping off the reddish 'winter' bark to reveal the lighter color beneath."

"How did you join the panels of bark together? I see you have bound them to the frame with twine of some sort," I observed.

"Those are sinews from the roots of the black spruce. When dried they make a strong, natural twine." Pointing to the gunwales the Wizard continued, "The Ojibway lashed the panels to the frame here, as you can see. The black sealant covers the seams of the birch-bark panels which are sewn together with the same sinews. The rest of the canoe—the frame, thwarts, ribs, and planking are all white cedar."

"It's a work of art," I commented admiringly, running my hand across one of the bark panels with its natural bumps and swirls.

"And also very functional," said the Wizard. "Art was very much a part of their lives. It was integrated into the whole fabric of their day-to-day existence, not something separate and apart, to admire in galleries, as it is for us. They lived very close to nature's bounty which gave them a deep reverence for all living things. With all our blacktop and air-conditioned shopping malls we no longer have a regular link with the natural world. We are alienated from our origins. This creates an imbalance in our lives that can only be offset by intentionally creating a closeness to nature. This is what canoeing can do. It is so soulfully satisfying."

"My life could use a little more of that soulful stuff."

"We all need it to bring our lives back into balance," said the Wizard. "Sounds as if stress is getting the best of you.

"I fear it is."

"When you think about stress, what comes to mind?" asked the Wizard.

"I think of ulcers, headaches, deadlines, high blood pressure, and things like that."

"That is a pretty negative list."

"You asked me what I thought about and that's how I see it—I don't like it."

"Are you excited about living?" the Wizard asked with a mischievous look.

"Why yes, why do you ask?"

"Considering the alternative, it is not so bad," smiled the Wizard. "If you are excited about life, you are excited about stress."

"You're saying excitement is stressful?" I asked.

"That is right. You cannot have excitement without stress. Do you enjoy competition?"

"I've always loved to compete both in sports and in business."

"If you love competition, you love stress."

"If you say so," I said, reluctantly conceding but not knowing where the Wizard's words were leading me.

"Tell me, are you eagerly anticipating your next intimate moment?" he asked with roguish glee.

"How can I say no? Don't tell me that is stressful!" I rejoined playfully, responding to the Wizard's mood.

"The key word is not what you think. It is *anticipating*. When we anticipate anything, we raise our stress level in preparation for the more stressful event which we are expecting. It is our way of getting ready so the body does not experience sudden, unexpected shock stress."

"So anticipation is stressful?" I reflected. "I suppose it's like turning up the heat gradually, rather than jumping into hot water."

"Right on!" exclaimed the Wizard. "In travel, getting there is said to be half the fun. This is the fun of anticipation."

"But that's fun. I would think anticipating something bad, like living in fear, would be more stressful."

"It is, but at the physiological level, it is all basically the same response. The stress response is commonly called the fight/flight syndrome."

"I've heard of that," I said showing some understanding. "When we see something we don't like, we either fight or flee. Right?"

"That is the general idea, but first we need to understand the difference between *stress* and *stressor*. Many people confuse the two. Stress is the body's physiological response to the stressor; whereas the stressor is the causal agent, the thought that causes the stress. Do you know what our most common stressor is?"

"Money?"

"No. People," replied the Wizard. "They are the source of our greatest frustrations and our greatest satisfactions."

"You're saying we can't live with them and we can't live without them."

"That is conventional wisdom, and there is some truth to it.

People make the greatest demands on us for change and that is what stress is all about," concluded the Wizard.

"Are you saying stress is a demand for change?"

"Simply stated, yes," affirmed the Wizard. "Stress is the body's reaction to any demand for change."

"So stress is the body's response to change?"

"Exactly. The physical symptoms you experience as a result of a stressor's action are your body's response to that demand. And that response is called the fight/flight syndrome."

"So the body is getting ready to fight or flee the stressor," I summarized. "Then if stress is the result of any demand for change, we must be feeling more stress than ever today in these times of rapid change."

"You are absolutely right. Stress is our legacy from a life of accelerating change. Here is how it works. When a stressor makes a demand on the body, the generic response is the fight/flight syndrome—blood pressure rises, heart and respiration rate rise, perspiration increases, oxygenated blood supply to the brain and to the large body muscles increases, blood sugar elevates, fatty acids release in blood, nostrils flare, throat dries out as salivary glands cease to function, etc. It is a state of alarm, a coordinated response of an aroused body to any disruptive situation or stimulus. The body is simply trying to preserve its internal stability."

"All that just for stability?"

"The body needs to stay in balance. The medical term for this is *homeostasis*. The term comes from two Greek words—the prefix *homoio* meaning similar or like, and the root word *sta* meaning standing. The body wants to 'stay like it is.' Good health and well-being begin with a body in homeostatic balance. For example, the body wants to stay at a temperature of 98.6 Fahrenheit. This is the norm. Relatively modest variations from this norm indicate abnormal conditions. So it is with countless other subtle indicators of a healthy body."

"But now you are talking about agents that raise the body's temperature like bacteria or viruses. I thought we were talking about people as stressors."

"Body stressors come in many forms—germs, toxins, drugs,

temperature changes, hard surfaces, sharp objects, offensive sights and sounds, and rude people. I simply said that people were our most common stressors. They alter our emotional state; that has instant physical effects."

"You mean that people cause us to be angry or frustrated and this upsets our balance."

"Yes. There are, however, two very key points here. The first is that stressors throw us out of balance and the body employs the fight/flight response to restore its stability. This is a very primitive response designed to get our internal 'house' in order. The body needs to maintain its internal stability and it takes emergency measures to do so. It prepares us to fight the stressor or to flee from it.

"The second point is of paramount importance. I cannot make this point too strongly. It is not what happens to us that hurts us, but rather how we take it."

"What do you mean by 'how we take it?'" I asked.

"We tend to blame stressors for our own inadequacies," mused the Wizard. "We love to externalize our problems, blame them on someone else. It is a very old game, but we will make very little personal progress until we overcome this human tendency to point the finger at someone else."

"Are you saying we should point the finger at ourselves?"

"That would be a very good start. One of the greatest thinkers of our time, Carl Jung, said, 'I have never encountered a difficulty that was not truly the difficulty of myself.'"

"But there are some people that really distress me, and you're saying that's my fault?"

"Let's not talk about whose fault it is, but rather say that you have other options. You do not need to be distressed."

"But I thought you said I couldn't help being distressed. The body is getting me ready to fight or flee, what other options are there?"

"Remember, the fight/flight response is a very primitive one, a state of alarm designed for life-threatening experiences. Today stressful experiences are more likely to threaten our self-esteems than our lives. The idea is to use the arousal energy for more useful purposes."

"Like what?"

"Have you ever experienced 'stage fright' as a speaker?"

"Yes," I replied. "Regularly."

"Stage fright is another name for the stress response. It is not appropriate, however, for the speaker to fight the audience or to flee from them, although the latter may be what you would like to do! So what do you do? You channel that energy into making a more animated presentation with timely hand gestures, body movements, facial expressions, and increased vocal emphasis. You take the attitude that nature is giving you greater energy to make your speech more interesting and effective. It is a gift."

"Stage-fright is a gift? That's a switch if I ever heard one."

"Stage-fright is not a gift, but the energy that you experienced as stage-fright is a gift. The key is to see it as a positive experience, a challenge. Call it 'stage-excitement' rather than stage-fright if you will, and use it as a gift. Attitude makes the difference. Again, it is not what happens to you that hurts you, it is how you take it.

"Let me put it to you more strongly," the Wizard continued. "You said some people cause you to be angry. That is not possible without your permission. I cannot make you angry, fearful, or frustrated. Nor can I make you feel guilty. I cannot even make you happy, unless. . . ."

"Unless what?"

"Unless you allow me to do so. It is your choice, not mine. You cannot always control the things that happen to you, but you can control how you respond to them. That is your call, and your options are as varied as your imagination. You can simply choose not to be upset. Instead, you may choose to be happy or indifferent, to change the subject, to offer a compromise, to thank the other person for her emotional honesty, to laugh or tell a story, to reciprocate with kindness. The options are endless. The point is: you do not have to be upset."

"That sounds so simple, but that takes a lot of self-control. I'm not sure I have that much poise."

"Remember, simple is seldom easy. Jung said 'It would be

simple enough, if only simplicity were not the most difficult of all things.'"

"I recall your saying that simple is not easy last time we met. Why is that so?"

"The human thing to do is to blame others, to externalize our problems. That is easy, but it does not work. We take the easy way out by refusing to see that the solutions lie within us. The simple solution is to accept personal responsibility for our own attitudes and behaviors and not point the finger at others, but that is not easy. It means I have to change and that raises my stress level. Once again Jung offers us an insight: 'Whatever we fight in the outside world is also a battle in our inner selves. . . . Anyone who can admit this will first seek the solution in himself, and this in fact is the way all the great solutions begin.'

"The idea here is that we are more alike than different. Therefore I can find the answers 'in here,' within myself, to problems I have with other people 'out there.'"

"When we first met you said if I came to you for answers that I had traveled in vain—that the answers I sought lay within me. This must be what you had in mind."

"You remember well. This is one example of how we can use the idea to help us manage our stress. If we don't take charge of our own stress response, our lives are literally out of control and our health is in jeopardy. Dr. Hans Selye, the great medical stress-research pioneer, taught us that our adaptation energy is finite and limited. Living with prolonged stress can literally deplete our deep energy reserves making us defenseless and vulnerable to a growing list of illnesses."

"This is all about managing my response to others. Isn't there something I can do before all this happens, something that might generally make my life more stress-free?" I implored.

"In his classic *Stress Without Distress* Selye says the key to avoiding harmful stress is first to choose an environment of work, family, and friends that provides optimal stress for ourselves. Notice, he said 'optimal stress,' not stress-free. Some people have a greater innate capacity to handle stress. Indeed, some thrive on it. Second, within that optimal environment, we must expend our energies on what gives us joy and self-respect. In other words, choose an appropriately stressful context for our lives and then make the content of our lives joyful and productive."

"That's a tall order, the kind of life that we all want but few achieve," I observed.

"It is also pretty basic, yet we need to remind ourselves regularly lest we forget. Selye urges us to 'earn thy neighbor's love' and to make ourselves as useful as possible because we can't afford to do otherwise. The consequences of not doing so are too costly."

"What a lovely thought that it's in our best interests to be useful to others, to earn their love. It's too bad more people don't realize this. That in helping others we are really doing ourselves a favor."

"I believe it is part of God's elegant design," said the Wizard. "Shakespeare said the quality of mercy is 'twice blessed; it blesseth him that gives and him that takes.' Helping someone else helps you as well. That is a double blessing."

"What I'm learning is that stress is not all bad. The determining factor is my attitude toward it. How can I be sure I have the right attitude?"

"There are many things we can do to insure that we are receptive to the demands of stress, but that will have to wait for another time. Remember for now that stress is neither good nor bad—like nature, it simply is. Distress is stress that affects us adversely. One of the reasons why we perceive stress negatively is because we do not have a common, generic word for positive stress. Selye gave us the word *eustress* (*Eu* is a Greek prefix meaning 'good.') but it has not caught on. Why not say it a few times to give it some help," the Wizard smiled.

"Eustress! Eustress! It sounds like a high school football cheer!"

"You make a good point. Eustress makes any game exciting. Life would be very dull without eustress. That was what I meant earlier when I talked about competition, excitement, and anticipation. We often associate burn-out with the distress brought on by overdoing. There is another more subtle malaise called 'rust-out,' which comes not from overdoing but from underbeing."

"Rust-out? Underbeing? What do you mean?"

"Not enough stimulation, insufficient challenge, prolonged tedium. For example, today a lot of people are rusting-out through underemployment. They simply are not challenged by their jobs, or they are performing tasks that are intrinsically unsatisfying.

"When our skills exceed the challenge, we are bored. When the challenge exceeds our skills, we are anxious. That is why it is so necessary to find a balance. This is what Selye had in mind when he talked about finding the right context for our lives so that we are optimally stressed, not distressed nor stress-free. To be stress-free is to be dead. I don't think that is what you had in mind."

"You're right about that. I'll not complain about stress again!"

"If we are mindful of a few basic considerations, we would experience considerably less distress and we could handle the demands of stress with greater equanimity. What is required are some lifestyle adjustments that many of us seem unwilling to make. It is a matter of trade-offs. That is the way life is."

Suggestions

The Wizard summarized some basics on stress management and then said we have, broadly speaking, only three choices for action:

Stress Summary

- Stress is the physical consequence of any demand made on the body.
- Much of our stress comes from problem relationships.
- If this stress is intense and prolonged, illnesses will result.
- The tendency is to blame the stressors, or sources of stress.
- The fact is, it is not what happens to you that hurts you,

but rather how you take it. In other words, your attitude is the key factor.

Choices

1. You may address the situation, confront the person who is the stressor in your life. This requires assertive, caring action. You simply describe the behavior you find unacceptable, preferably immediately after it happens, and relate how it makes you feel. Avoid making judgments and suggest to the other person how you wish to be treated if this relationship is to grow.
2. You may separate yourself from the other person. If you choose this option, do so joyfully. Separation with malice and recrimination is not an acceptable alternative.
3. You may choose to live with the situation. This requires acceptance and forgiveness. These two criteria are essential. Wallowing in misery is not acceptable. Dr. Norm Shealy calls this "going for sainthood."

• Identify a relationship problem that you have, make your choice, and take the necessary action. Your body will thank you for it.

3
The Big Four of
Stress Reduction

Having a purpose is the difference between
making a living and making a life.

I tried to think more positively about stress in the time
between my visits with the Wizard. As always my days were
filled with stressful thoughts and events. It was hard for me
to realize that all these feelings I experienced were positive.
Then I remembered that the Wizard said stage-fright itself
was not a gift, but the energy surge that I experienced from
stage fright was a gift. If I could only direct those energy
bursts toward more positive ends. Turning *distress* into
eustress is an art I had yet to master. Attitude, he said, is the
key. Then I remembered a couplet from Kipling:

"If you can meet Triumph and Disaster
And treat those two impostors just the same. . . ."

How to meet those two impostors, distress and eustress,
and treat them just the same—as a gift. That is the challenge!
I was keen to hear about those lifestyle adjustments that the
Wizard talked about. What trade-offs would I have to consider? Would I be open to making those changes? Fortunately,
it was not long before I saw the Wizard again. He was in his
garden planting.

"What are you growing this summer?" I asked.

"Lots of good things—corn, beans, squash, carrots, lettuce, sprouts, melons, tomatoes, kale, . . ."

"Kale?"

"It's a cabbage-like vegetable, rich in vitamins and minerals," said the Wizard. "I can't guarantee you would like it, but your body would."

"Last time you talked about some lifestyle adjustments, is kale one of them?" I asked in jest.

The Wizard laughed. "Only if you want it to be. Some things you have to develop a taste for."

"I never understood why I should develop a taste for something I didn't like. Take coffee, for instance. I've never liked the taste. Friends would say, 'Oh, it's an acquired taste. You'll learn to like it.' Why should I acquire a taste for something I don't like?"

"I can't fault your reasoning. You are lucky you don't like coffee. That is our number one addiction. Surely, however, there are things you like now that you didn't care for as a child. Some tastes just change over time. I used to cull mushrooms out of my foods. Now I seek them out."

"I never liked them as a child either."

"Mushrooms have unique chemistries," asserted the Wizard, "that produce compounds not found elsewhere in nature. In America, we have not explored these properties. Mushrooms have been part of the natural pharmacopoeias of China and Japan for ages. In Asia many are cultivated, sold in markets, and reported to have great health benefits—lowering cholesterol and blood sugar, preventing cancer, and so on. Some contain large molecules called *polysaccharides,* which may have anti-viral and anti-tumor properties with their ability to stimulate the immune response. The best known in America is the shiitake—"*

"I am reminded," I interrupted, "of what a little girl said when asked what she thought about a book on penguins. She said, 'This book tells me more about penguins than I care to know!'"

* The Wizard is indebted to Dr. Andrew Weil for this insight.

The Wizard laughed uproariously. "Sorry about that. I do get carried away sometimes. Thanks for telling me so gently what I needed to know."

"No offense intended," I said. "That was rather rude of me. Actually, I greatly admire your interest and your knowledge. That's just my way of covering up for my inadequacies. I couldn't pass up the opportunity to tease you. The message you're telling me, I presume, is to eat more fresh vegetables. What if I don't like them?"

"You can acquire a taste," the Wizard replied, grinning broadly.

With that, I laughed knowing we had come full circle.

"Vegetables, yes, but more fruits and whole grains too. *Diet*. That is the first of the big four of stress reduction—diet, exercise, relaxation, and living a purposeful life."

"What has diet to do with stress reduction?" I asked.

"It may well be the most important factor. We need to prepare the body to take the stress 'hits.' Remember, stress is a demand for change imposed upon the body. A healthy body can take a lot more stress. If you are eating the right things, are physically fit, have a wide repertoire of relaxation methods, and lead a purposeful life, you are nearly immune to distress.

"We pride ourselves on our health care system but in truth we do not have one. We have a disease management system with only 3% of the budget spent on prevention. That is not health care. We have designed an acute, traumatic disease management system for a nation that is suffering from chronic illnesses, and we have not made much progress on those."

"What do you mean by chronic illnesses?"

"If you have an emergency, this is great system to care for you, but if you have cancer, heart disease, adult-onset diabetes, or one of the auto-immune diseases our record is not very good. These are the chronic, life-style diseases that usually emerge later in life. In his book, *Sound Mind, Sound Body,* Dr. Kenneth Pelletier reports a 1990 study of the Surgeon General who listed twenty-one major causes of illness and death. Nineteen were 'entirely lifestyle related—the result of destructive lifestyle choices.' Regardless of what you hear, we are not winning the war on cancer. From the mid-1970s to the early 1990s the incidence of cancer rose 18.6% for men and 12.4% for women. Furthermore, there has been little change since the 1930's in the survival rate of adults with cancer tumors. Contrary to popular opinion, genetics plays a minor role in most chronic illnesses. Lifestyle is the key and diet is a major risk factor. Our celebrated Western standard of living has not produced a very healthful diet. It suffers from 'the too's'—too much fat, too much sugar, too much salt, and too much refined flour."

"And too few fresh fruits, vegetables, and whole grains," I added.

"That is the sum of it. The word 'vegetable' derives from the Latin *vegetare* which means 'to quicken or enliven.' Many top triathlon athletes are on a low fat, high carbohydrate diet because it enlivens them. They see a difference in their performance.

"Even ordinary people who have made the change almost invariably report an increase in energy. This energy increase usually leads to a more active life which is the second consideration—*exercise*. Diet and exercise go together. Neither can carry the load alone. Our sedentary lifestyle combined with our American diet has been a killer."

"But aren't we doing better in this area?"

"Better than in the diet arena. In addition to the fitness benefits, exercise lowers blood pressure, raises HDL's (high-density lipoproteins), and strengthens the immune system. A sedentary lifestyle suppresses the immune function making us more susceptible to disease.

"I think the general awareness of the public has been raised, but the majority remain literally unmoved. Look around you; you don't need to read the statistics to see that we are a nation that eats too much and exercises too little. Obesity has reached epidemic proportions in America. One third of all adults are obese! Worse yet, one fifth of all children are obese! Obesity means at least 20% above the recommended weight range. A Harris Poll found a staggering

71% of Americans are overweight, 79% of the men and 64% of the women.

"Walking 20 minutes a day at an easy pace of three mph (20 minute mile) will burn about 100 calories. At that rate, do you know how long it will take to burn off one pound of fat—not water, but fat?"

"No, how long?"

"Five weeks! (3500 calories to lose one pound of fat.) Losing or gaining solid weight is a steady, slow process. There are no tricks, no quick ways that are healthful. The process is simply calorie intake minus calorie outgo. If you eat 2400 calories per day and expend 2300. Your body will store those 100 unused calories in fat cells. If you do that every day for 35 days you will weigh one pound more. Fat accumulates as much from underdoing as from overeating. That is why regular exercise is so vital a part of good health."

"That's amazing. No wonder people give up exercising when they don't see results right away."

"I believe the fitness boom in recent years was largely stress-induced," said the Wizard, "rather than any real desire to improve health."

"What do you mean by that?" I asked.

"One of the best ways of dissipating stress is through exercise. That sudden state of energy arousal that comes from stress requires that we expend it in some physical way. People discovered that they felt better after exercising. They were less tense, they felt more positive about themselves, and they were more balanced and better able to deal with their problems. Ideally, our stress level would rise with the challenges we face at work and it would dissipate as we worked through them. Unfortunately, it doesn't always work this way.

"We may come to work with a stress load of unresolved tension making it difficult for us to handle the demands of work. Further unresolved issues at work may compound this stress and we go home with greater stress at the end of the day. This is a cycle that can only be broken with conscious stress-reduction methods."

"Like what?"

"Like exercise. This is one unspoken reason why companies sponsor employee sports and health club memberships. It helps reduce the tensions of the day. You are less likely to come home and snap at the kids after nine innings of softball—especially if you win! Furthermore, after exercise you are more receptive to *relaxation,* the third consideration in stress management."

"This is an area I need help in," I admitted. "I recall your saying the last time we met that the answers I sought would come when I was in a relaxed state, that I couldn't force them, and that trying didn't help. That was a revelation to me."

"Would you like to go canoeing?"

"I'd love to!" With that we walked over to a small outbuilding, lifted the birch-bark canoe off its sawhorses, and carried it to a small lake scarcely a hundred yards away. The Wizard steadied the canoe as I got in. He told me to keep my weight centered and low as I crept toward the bow. He then shoved off and effortlessly settled into the stern. I was struck with how serene the setting was. We glided silently for a few minutes before he spoke.

"Life is a continuous cycle of energy expenditure and recovery. Not only do we waste much of our vital energy with unproductive distress, but we also do not allow ourselves ample time to recover, to regenerate ourselves. That is the purpose of recreation, to 're-create' ourselves. We are a nation of busybodies and the true benefits of relaxation continue to elude us. It is a hangover from the defunct Puritan ethic that built our industrial capacity and compelled us to work continuously and to defer our rewards. We spend so much time doing that we do not know how *not to do.*

"I feel guilty when I'm not doing something."

"That is the challenge—how not to do without guilt. The first consideration is to make certain we are getting enough sleep. My mother used to tell me when I had a problem that I would feel better in the morning after a good night's sleep. I thought that advice had nothing to do with my immediate problem and I resisted it, but she was right. Many of us suffer from sleep deprivation, inadequate or insufficient rest from doing too much. The quality of our doing deteriorates rapidly with fatigue.

"Furthermore research shows that when you sleep less you eat more and more often, and that contributes to our growing obesity. We simply have to get better at not doing."

"You're advocating doing nothing?"

"No, on the contrary. Not doing something is different from doing nothing. Not doing is a deliberate choice not to do, which is doing something! That something is not doing."

"Ah, Wizard, you always have the last word. What would you have me *not do*?"

"I would have you *be*." he said, raising his eyebrows with anticipatory wonderment.

"Be?"

"Yes, in our rush to do we have lost the gentle art of being. Being is our essence, our spirit, our essential nature. I would suggest you get in touch with your being."

"How do I do that?" I asked.

"Simply experience the moment. Focus totally on what is happening at this precise moment. It might be the sound of the quaking aspen leaves, the changing patterns of wind on the water, the honking of Canadian geese searching for nesting grounds in the boggy marshland offshore, the sight of ever-evolving cloud formations, or the effortless soaring of a solitary hawk. Concentrate on watching what happens rather than making something happen. Pass no judgments, just observe fully, with all your senses.

By now I had stopped paddling and was just taking in the full experience. He continued. "Feel the warmth of the sun and the different temperature changes as we glide into the shade and out again; smell the air and the subtle scents that waft by; watch the little wind squalls that first appear as a shallow agitation on the water's surface and feel its gentle force as it passes through you; put your hand in the water and savor the cooling effect of evaporation as you 'hang it out to dry' in the sun. For the moment, just be the sentient being you were designed to be."

I don't know how long I was silent but it seemed forever.

Then I spoke, "I was going to ask, 'What will this do for me?' but I now know. It's very calming, isn't it?"

"It is," affirmed the Wizard. "Remember homeostasis? You are coming back into balance. This will enhance your power of awareness which is the meditative art. Furthermore, when you come back into the *doing* realm later, the quality of your doing will improve. Being has restorative powers and you can *be* anywhere, anytime. Canoeing just makes it easier."

"It's really dropping out, wouldn't you say?"

"It is like dropping out for a moment, but in truth you are dropping in—dropping into the heart of your being and savoring life itself which lives only in the moment. We live, laugh, and love only in the present and then it is gone only to be replaced by another present moment, and another, ad infinitum. The art is staying in the present with no worries of the past nor concerns of the future. It is very relaxing and empowering for the spirit."

"I can feel it."

"There are many things you can do to relax when you don't have access to a setting like this. Taking a few deep breaths through your nose does wonders. The fight/flight response is a rapid, shallow breath. You can offset this with some slow, deep breathing through the nose. Just doing this alone before taking any action can be very calming.

"There are also many beneficial ways of dropping out. Work breaks, weekends, holidays, and vacations are all legal 'drop-outs.' You can add to these with imaginative journeys. Simply close your eyes and visualize a favorite restful place— a stretch of solitary beach, an alpine meadow, a pine forest path, a mountaintop view, a field of wild flowers. Better yet, come back in your mind to this moment and recreate this setting in the canoe with your mind's eye. Feel it fully with all your senses and return to the wakeful world when ready."

No sooner had he said "ready" than I noticed we had come full circle as he nosed the canoe gently into the soft grasses along the shoreline. We disembarked as carefully as we embarked, pulled the canoe up farther on shore, and walked back to the garden.

Picking up where he left off while on the lake he said, "That is the beauty of imagination. All relaxation methods are maintenance acts designed to offset the hustle of daily affairs. To take charge of our lives more fully and to give them direction and meaning, however, we need to address our *purpose*. This is the fourth dimension of stress management." With that the Wizard stopped, faced me squarely, and asked with great intensity, "What is your purpose in life?"

The depth and suddenness of the question jarred me, to say nothing of his somewhat confrontive stance. "I don't know. I never really thought about it," I replied, pausing for reflection "I suppose it's to make a decent living and to raise my family to be responsible adults."

"What about yourself?" The Wizard probed. "Are you through with yourself now that you are putting all your energies into your family?"

"Why no, I . . . I don't think so," I replied, stammering a bit. "I don't know. I haven't had the time to think about myself lately."

"You are not alone. Most of us have given little thought to it. Isn't it curious? We spend more time planning a vacation than we do our lives. We say we don't have the time but, in truth, we have not taken the time. We have time for what is important to us. Purpose has just not made the top-ten on our priority list."

The Wizard leaned closer to me and locked his eyes on mine. "One of the great things about a purposeful life is that it enables you to say 'no.' Many of us are distressed—stretched beyond our limits—because we take too much on. We can't say 'no.' Having a clear purpose enables you to say 'no' to those things that do not fit your purpose—and to say 'yes' to those that do. A purposeful life provides a positive attitude which is the nexus that holds all the other elements together. Having a purpose is the difference between making a living and making a life. Most of us put all our energies into making a living at the expense of making a life.

"We often confuse the two. Making a living is a subset of making a life. If your purpose is in concert with the universe, if it edifies and ennobles the human spirit, you will be making a life—and making a living will follow. Any moments of distress will be overwhelmed with the sheer volume of energy and goodwill you bring to the experience. I promise you."

I could feel the intensity of his words. The energy he exuded was palpable. I didn't know what to say. What could I say to add to that? I simply felt a mixture of serenity and power that I had not experienced before. It was intoxicating.

Moving away, the Wizard matter-of-factly said, "Well there you have it, the big four of stress management—diet, exercise, relaxation, and a clear sense of purpose. I am certain if we spend more time together we will have a lot more to say about all this. In the meantime, I have some planting to do. A garden is a wonderful metaphor for life, and for managing as well. In the words of Samuel Butler, 'For as you sow, ye are like to reap.' That is the way life is."

Suggestions

The Wizard had some additional thoughts in these four areas:

Diet

Diets do not work but a general move toward more natural foods—fruits, vegetables, and whole grains—does work. As you move gradually in this direction, observe your energy level. Listen to your body, not just your palate. Sugar, salt, and fat are the big three additives that cause most of the problems. Anybody can make food flavorful with enough of these. Challenge yourself to find and prepare foods that not only taste good but are good for you.

Begin by cutting your total fat intake, especially saturated fat. Saturated fat is found mostly in animal products It also is the principle cause for excess cholesterol in the body. Cholesterol is a major risk factor in heart disease and a disputed factor in some forms of cancer. Recent studies have proven that a diet very low in fat combined with exercise and meditative practices can actually reverse coronary heart disease. It will also keep the pounds off. More immediately, you will have increased energy.

Exercise

Physical activity is the only variable that you control to burn off calories over and above those needed for essential body functions. You use about 60% of your energy (calories) to sustain the heart, lungs, and all other body maintenance functions. This is your resting or basal metabolism. Your body uses another 10% for digestion. So far, you have used 70% of your available energy and all you've done is lift your fork! Any calorie intake over this essential amount that is not burned in physical activity will be stored as fat. How physically active you are with the remaining 30% of your energy is your choice. If your calorie input exceeds your calorie output (activity) you gain weight. It is that simple. In time, if your food choices remain the same while your metabolism and physical activity slow with age, obesity awaits you.

Some people have a more active metabolism and can burn calories more readily than others. For example, lean muscle tissue burns more calories than fat tissue. Exercise can burn off fat, but not cholesterol. Most important, a healthy and fit body is more alive, more responsive to life. The body is our sensing device allowing us to see, hear, smell, touch, and taste. We are sentient beings. That is, we are finely sensitive to feelings and perceptions. Good health heightens this capacity.

Begin with something simple. For those not into the more vigorous regimens, try walking. Many of the runners of the 80's are walkers in the 90's due to injuries. Read Casey Meyer's book *Walking* (see bibliography) and many of you will find you won't need much else. If you want to supplement your walking regimen with increased flexibility and stability, do yoga. Stretching will help, but yoga has the added benefits of meditative practice, balance, and strength training as well. We feel old when we lose mobility in our joints. Yoga will restore the fuller range of motion that is your body's birthright.

Relaxation

The options here are endless. Begin by making certain you are getting adequate sleep. Your body will tell you if you are not. Listen to it.

Learn your symptoms of distress. Headaches? Irritability? Lack of concentration? Short temper? Indecision? Restlessness? You will have your own unique constellation of characteristics that display your duress.

When you feel them, determine what stressor(s) caused them. If it is a relationship, deal with it in one of the three ways the Wizard suggested in the last chapter.

If it is something else, you may want to 'drop out' briefly to 'drop-in' to a state of relaxation so you may return later better prepared to deal with your issues. You can drop out three ways: physically by removing yourself, mentally by distraction, or chemically by medication. Taking a break to center yourself and clear your thinking is always in order. The only justification for taking most of the medication sold as stress relief, however, is to decrease your tension in order that you may 'buy' time to address the stressor later under more favorable conditions.

Medication, as with any drug, does not teach you coping skills. It only relieves symptoms. If every time you have a problem you pop a pill, you are not addressing the cause of the problem and are not learning responsible ways of coping. Thus most chemical stress relievers, including alcohol and cigarettes, are only *palliatives,* temporary pain relievers. Ultimately you must deal with the cause if you want to resolve distressing issues and move on in life.

Proper diet and exercise minimize the need for relaxation techniques because the effect of the stressors on a healthy body will not be as deleterious.

Practice being fully present in the moment as the Wizard demonstrated in the chapter. Lose yourself in the moment concentrating fully on some natural occurrence. Notice the calming effect it has on the body. Be aware of your changing symptoms such as heart and respiration rate as your body returns to balance. Then reapproach the stressful situation with renewed strength and confidence.

Find a quiet place, close your eyes, and take an imaginary trip to a place that makes you feel peaceful and refreshed. Again, monitor your body's signs such as your hands warming and your breath slowing as your symptoms of distress dissipate.

Purpose

You can eat all the right things, do your exercises dutifully, employ all the relaxation methods, and still be at loose ends with yourself if your life has no direction. Purpose gives direction. Goals are targets along the way but purpose is the way. Purpose perseveres and prevails with a positivism that sweeps aside the doubts and carries the day.

Ask yourself the question: What is my purpose in life? Write down your thoughts as they come. Don't worry about how noble or profound your thoughts are. Live with them for a time and then ask the question again. Living with the question is more important than getting immediate answers.

Mind and matter are one. Attitude is the golden thread that links all the health measures together. How is your attitude?

Begin by waking up and expressing gratitude for all that life has to offer. Take the attitude that everything that happens to you is a gift, especially the bad stuff. Look for the lesson in it and express your gratitude for it.

When you feel you need a lift, give your body a break and do something for someone else, and do it joyfully. See what it does to your spirits. Remember Selye's maxim: "Earn thy neighbor's love."

Be hopeful. To be hopeful is to desire something with a positive expectation of outcome.

If things don't turn out as you hope, accept it as a gift. Search for the lesson in the turn of events and move on with renewed hope.

4
Wholeness, Healing, and Habits

My role is to comfort the afflicted
and to afflict the comfortable.

Several weeks passed before I saw the Wizard again. I wanted to give the big four elements of stress reduction a fair chance. My diet had been a disaster. This was the hardest element to change but I was beginning to enjoy the natural flavor of foods again without the heavy additive doses of "the too's"—fat, sugar, salt, and refined flour. My heightened awareness had made meal preparation and eating more challenging and interesting.

As for exercise, I made a point to walk up stairs when available and began to develop a brisk walking routine. I also signed up for a yoga class and found some relief for a back problem that had defied other remedial efforts

Yoga also had helped me with relaxation because it required my conscious awareness at all times. To an outside observer it is just another stretching routine. To a yoga practitioner, however, it is the total alignment of mind and body. I had no idea it was so technically demanding. To this day I have found nothing to equal it for balance, flexibility, and strength.

I had also made it a habit to drop out as needed by "dropping in" as the Wizard suggested and use those quiet meditative moments to re-create myself.

After giving purpose a great deal of thought for a few weeks, I decided my purpose in life was to help others help themselves. I saw that the beauty of helping others was that in doing so, I was also helping myself. We used to call this "enlightened self-interest." This was what the Wizard was doing for me, helping me to become more responsible for myself. I began to see that that is what pastoral care is all about. As the Wizard had said when we first met, this is the "priesthood of management." That is what I had begun at work and it's what I had always tried to do at home.

The next time we met the Wizard was in his garden. Leaning on his hoe and looking pleased to see me, he inquired, "Did you ever see the stage play, *The Fantasticks?*"

"No, I didn't."

"In the 1960s, it was the longest-running production in American theatrical history. One of the reasons for this, I believe, was its simplicity. There is a delightful duet about growing vegetables that Huck and Bell sing in the second act."

Using a small trowel as a baton and the garden as a stage, the Wizard strutted along the plant rows and addressed each plant in song:

Plant a radish, get a radish.
Never any doubt.
That's why I love vegetables;
You know what you're about.

Plant a turnip, get a turnip.
Maybe you'll get two.
That's why I love vegetables;
You know that they'll come through!

They're dependable!
They're befriendable!
They're the best pal a parent's ever known!
While with children—
It's bewilderin'

You don't know until the seed is nearly grown,
Just what you've sown.

So . . .
Plant a carrot,
Get a carrot,
Not a brussels sprout.
That's why I love vegetables;
You know what you're about!

"Encore! More!" I shouted, applauding.

The Wizard blushed, suddenly self-conscious about his exuberant performance. "Thank you. I've always enjoyed the lyrics and the music in that play. It was very popular during the turbulent sixties when parents didn't know what was happening to their children, to the social order, to their cherished traditions, and to themselves. It struck a chord somewhere deep within us."

The Wizard went back to his hoeing. "Gardening is a healing art," he said. "Do you enjoy gardening?"

"I'm not a gardener," I replied.

"If you manage people, then you are a gardener."

"A gardener of people?"

"A gardener of *potential.* Belief in another person's potential is the most empowering thing you can do as a manager. Remember *The Wizard of Oz?* The Wizard gave courage, a heart, and wisdom to Dorothy's friends by merely affirming their potential. Gardeners and managers do the same thing. They both nurture potential.

"In nature, a seed is genetically programmed to become something. That something is already determined. Enfolded within the seed is the potential of how to be. Our job is to provide the appropriate context for it to unfold, to express that being, to release what is. That is the optimal stress setting that Selye urged us to find. It is really quite simple, as simple as tending a garden," said the Wizard.

"But if everything was so easy, then I wouldn't be here."

"Remember, simple is seldom easy. First you must take an

inner journey of self-awareness to find out who you are." Placing his hands over his heart, the Wizard paused. He then released his hands in an open gesture of giving. "Then you bring that sense of how to be into everything you do. That's what living is all about. Sadly, few people are willing to make that inner journey."

"You're really just telling me to find out what I do best and then do it," I said, in my most pragmatic manner.

The Wizard responded with a hesitant, "Yes . . . for now that will have to do."

"You don't sound convinced."

"Like a plant that grows from a seed to full flower, there are stages in the evolution of our being. I am content that your understanding of what I am saying is sufficient for now. You are on an inner journey, or you would not be here, and you must take it simultaneously with the outer journey."

"There are two journeys?" I asked, somewhat puzzled.

"Yes. The outer journey is the visible one, how we live our lives. The reason for the inner one is to open ourselves up to the mystery of life, to give purpose and meaning to the outer journey. It is a journey of the spirit, a path to our being, a how-to-be discovery voyage to reveal the essence of what we are. That's what is."

"I see where you get your nickname, the 'Wizard of Is.' "

"Potentially, we are all wizards because people, like plants, will become something with or without help. That is where managing a business, like gardening, can make a difference. The difference is in the quality of that becoming."

"Quality!" I said, my face brightening. "Now that's a word I hear a lot about in business today."

"I am talking about the authentic quality of living a whole life, about being who you are by developing what *is*," the Wizard said. "Just as the seed is qualitatively no less than the bud, and the bud is no less than the flower, the child is no less than the adult, the apprentice no less than the master. Each is complete at a certain stage while still evolving to the next level. Even so, we are all incomplete in terms of our qualitative potential.

"The manager, like the gardener, must intervene to assist as needed in this natural process of growth. It is tough for seeds to germinate on barren soil or to break through an asphalt overlay, and it is difficult for people to grow when the conditions for qualitative growth are not present. Often, however, in spite of great handicaps, people prevail."

"During our first visit we talked about healing in terms of wholeness," I recalled. "I've thought a lot about it, and you're right. When doctors heal, they make us whole again."

"Doctors do not heal," replied the Wizard, gently but authoritatively.

"They don't?" I must have looked somewhat surprised.

"Doctors only assist the healing process. The same is true with the manager and the parent and the gardener," said the Wizard. "God heals. Nature heals. The body, mind, and spirit heal. Healing is a natural process and wholeness is the natural state. It is unnatural to be fragmented."

"I suppose you're right. I see now why they call you the Wizard!"

"I am glad I was not living in this country 300 years ago," observed the Wizard.

"Why's that?"

"Did you know that at the celebrated Salem witch trials in 1692, both women and men were put to death? And a male witch was called a wizard. This wizard stuff was risky business! Fortunately, times have changed, but it is curious how the two words have evolved—to be a witch today is still not considered positive by most people, but to be a wizard, or even a whiz—that is all very good."

"I certainly don't think of wizards and witches in the same context."

"Language influences us more than we realize." The Wizard was now in his element, the world of words. "Men often come out sounding better in the language of our male-dominated culture. When a man loses his sexual power, we say he is impotent. When the same condition happens to a woman, we say she is frigid. In using these words, society defines a man in terms of power and a woman in terms of tempera-

Wholeness, Healing, and Habits   **39**

ture.* This means that men are supposed to be powerful and women are supposed to be warm. Why not warm men and powerful women?"

"I never thought of it that way," I admitted.

"Few people do. Our role as managers," said the Wizard, "is to awaken others. If I have awakened something within you, then I am pleased. My role is to comfort the afflicted and to afflict the comfortable. Healing requires both."

I noted the impish grin on the Wizard's face. "What do you mean by 'afflicting the comfortable'?"

The Wizard picked up his pruning shears and gently snipped several small shoots off a young apple tree. Looking down at the shears in his hands, the Wizard said, "A doctor has many tools to facilitate the healing process. The harshest of these is the scalpel. It hurts when it cuts, but it is a healing instrument. Surgery, although it destroys, can expedite the healing process. As a gardener, we have to snip off some branches to give a tree shape and boost its growth. Sometimes as managers or as parents we have to take 'surgical' action to change behavior.

"If you would like to understand what I mean by 'afflicting the comfortable,' it helps to know a bit about habit. Simply speaking, habits are patterns of behavior formed by our brain, the greatest patterning instrument ever devised. William James said that 'habit is the enormous flywheel of society, its most precious conservative agent.' That metaphor illustrates the power of habit."

"Interesting," I said, puzzled. "I don't think of the brain as a habit-making device."

"The brain's most undervalued talent is its capacity to pattern," said the Wizard. "Patterns make things familiar and understandable for us. Without patterns, life would have no meaning."

"What kind of patterns?"

As the Wizard spoke, he tied up some errant sweet pea sprouts to a lattice of string. "The brain organizes the information it receives into patterns of perception that make sense

* The Wizard is indebted to Sam Keen for this insight.

to us. This is what makes things familiar. We then act on the basis of these perceptions. When our actions are repeated, they become habits or routines. The brain is at its uncreative best when it is acting habitually in its tried and proven ways. This is the flywheel, our most precious conservative agent."

"What do you mean by 'uncreative best'?"

"If the brain were not so brilliant in this ability to make things familiar to us, every experience we have would be new. Nothing would be familiar. Can you imagine how that would be? You couldn't have found your way here today, and you certainly would never find your way home. You would have no recollection of it, but it would not matter anyway—when you got home you would not recognize your own family!"

We both laughed at the absurdity of it all.

"And to think we take this all for granted," I said, throwing my arms in the air.

"Yes, that is why I say the brain is undervalued. We do not accord it the recognition it deserves. This brilliant ability, however, is also the brain's greatest limitation."

"How's that?"

"Habit patterns become routines, and routines become ruts. When life is a rut, we act without thought. We become mindless, unaware, and out of touch with the present. We become trapped in a mindset. No longer mindful of the moment, we lose that special feeling of aliveness that was so present in the canoe last time we met. Then we are, for all intents, dead."

"Dead?"

"Dead to the present, the only state in which we live," clarified the Wizard. "Therefore, dead to life. We exist, but we do not live. We are not alive to life. We are in our 'comfort zone,' a complacent satisfaction with things as they are. We are reluctant to try something new, to 'test our edges.' In a rapidly changing world, this can be fatal."

"So what are we to do?" I asked. "What can I do?"

"We have to jar the brain out of its comfortable mindset, or life will jar it for us. We are often the last to realize when our habits no longer serve us well," explained the Wizard. "This is what I call 'afflicting the comfortable.'"

"But how can I jar my brain?"

"We have to jar our senses, jar our awareness, and jar our perception. To grow, we have to break out of these self-imposed, comfortable mindsets. This will heighten our awareness and put our senses on maximum alert. Then we will experience the feeling of aliveness once again." The Wizard opened his arms expansively and drew a deep, satisfying breath. "It's like going outside and breathing fresh air after being cooped up in a room for days."

"I need some of that fresh air, so how do I go about it?" I pressed.

"Aliveness comes from seeing and doing things differently. This is the essence of creativity. Creative artists see the world differently and interpret it through the media of paint, lyrics, music, photography, or dance. The enduring ones are those who change with the times. This is how they stay alive artistically. They have cultivated what Ellen Langer calls 'creative uncertainty,' and that enables them to stay tuned to the present. To keep breathing fresh air they must forever fend off the negative forces of habit."

"So now we're back to habit," I said with resignation in my voice.

"Remember," reminded the Wizard, "that's the flywheel, what the brain does best. The way we see things determines the way we do things. And the way we do things, in turn, influences how we see things. This forms a mindset, a closed habit loop of seeing things repeatedly in the same way and acting accordingly: If we always do what we always did, we'll always get what we always got. Breaking out of this mindset, or comfort zone, is difficult because it is uncomfortable. Habits persist unless we afflict our comfortable ways."

"How do you suggest we afflict ourselves?" I asked, rather fearful of the Wizard's possible answers.

"One way to set habits aside is to address old situations in new ways. A good method is to put yourself in unfamiliar situations. For example, traveling or living in a foreign culture will help you take a fresh look at your old ways. We do not have to go abroad, however, to find unfamiliar situations.

Any new challenge will do. Start a new hobby, seek out new friends, take a different kind of vacation, do something daring . . ."

"Daring? Like what?"

"Last year for my birthday," the Wizard paused as he cocked his head to one side and shifted his eyes upward, "I went skydiving for the first time."

I went slackjawed. "Skydiving! What was it like?"

"I have never experienced a similar sense of aliveness. When you step out of an airplane two miles up, tumble out into space, and fall 7,000 feet in 35 seconds, you experience a sensory assault quite unlike anything you ever felt before."

"But why did you do it?"

"I wanted to test my edges. I was curious as to how I would react to the challenge. That is the 'creative uncertainty' I mentioned. In this sport, you really have to stay focused on the present. I had no idea how I would feel when the door opened at an altitude of 10,500 feet and the jumpmaster said, 'Let's go!' "

I looked at the Wizard with a mixture of awe and wonderment. "Skydiving is really quite safe, just unforgiving of mistakes." The Wizard chuckled. "At that height, you are approximately one minute from impact with the ground. That tends to focus your attention on the moment."

"I should think so," I exclaimed.

"But the point is, try to put yourself in unfamiliar situations. Another way to break habits is to enlarge the context in which you live and work. This is called *reframing*. The environmental slogan, 'Think Globally, Act Locally,' illustrates this. If we enlarge our frame of reference to think of the global consequences of our actions, we are likely to change the way we behave at the local level. Our reframed view may alter what we do. This is what we call the big picture. Seeing this larger view often afflicts our comfortable ways, however, and we do not make changes. We wait until things get intolerably bad before we break our habits. Then, like the alcoholic who loses a job and a family before taking treatment, we reluctantly change."

"I must be in one of those habit loops," I said with resignation. "My life is out of my control. I go from crisis to crisis. I'm not managing my staff very well. I'm just reacting to things, putting out the fires. It's very frustrating."

Holding up his index finger, the Wizard predicted, "If you make just one change, your work habits will change significantly. I am talking about the need for you to understand the fundamental differences between urgency and importance."

"In my world," I retorted, "there is no difference. Everything is urgent and important."

"That is precisely the perception we will break, but that must wait until our next meeting. Now I must attend to my garden. Its full fruition is fast approaching. These plants are destined to bring forth their bounty and I want to facilitate that process." The Wizard looked at me and winked. "This is not unlike raising children, you know. They need me at this stage in their development. The outcome will be so much more rewarding if I help them now. That is the way life is."

Suggestions

Here are some of the things the Wizard had me do.

Experiment with your routines by changing them. Begin by focusing on one. Change the time, the location, the people, the duration, and/or the agenda. Observe what happens to your level of awareness. Likewise, observe what happens to your energy level.

At work, at home or at play, add an unfamiliar dimension to your familiar procedures:

1. Take a different vacation—at a different place, with different people, or at a different time.
2. Invite an outsider to a meeting of regular insiders.
3. Discuss a subject that isn't normally talked about.
4. Arrange the chairs in a circle; rearrange the furniture.
5. Let someone else moderate a meeting you would normally be in charge of.

6. Form self-managing work teams.
7. Question all routines, procedures, and reports. Challenge each person to practice "creative uncertainty" by doing things differently in a manner that will make a difference.
   • Make an effort to see the bigger picture. Reframe things in a larger context and observe how your options increase.
   • Seek ways to comfort those who feel afflicted and to "afflict" those who feel too comfortable.
   • Think of yourself as a gardener of potential. What can you contribute to this garden of diversity to increase its yield?
   • See yourself as a benevolent Wizard of Oz who affirms the potential of each person differently.
   • Be a "greedy" listener. Listen for the feelings as well as the facts. Listening for feelings will free up emotional blockages and release energy for more useful purposes. Few people have ever been criticized for listening too much.

Talk about the dislocations, challenges, and tensions these changes caused, as well as the positive outcomes. What does this say about you, the people you work with, or the other members of your family?

What does this say about your tolerance, your adaptability, your resourcefulness?

Ask "what if" questions to stimulate anticipatory thinking:

1. What if you were given a free hand to do what you thought best for your company?
2. What if you had a magic wand that allowed you to make one change in your work life? What would it be?
3. What if your staff could promote or demote you? What changes do you think you would want to make?
4. What if your children could give you a performance review? What grade, A through F, would they give you, and what would you do differently as a result?
5. What if your best customer gave you 30 days to improve service or lose the account?

6. What if your mate put you on 30 day notice? What would the charges be and what would you do about them?
7. What would you do differently if you could start your career over again?
8. What if you had only one year to live? How would your priorities change?
9. What if you won the lottery? How would you spend $10 Million?

5
Making the Important Urgent

You can no longer be just a problem solver.
You must also become a possibility seeker.

In the days that followed, I tried to do some things differently. I varied my route to work in the morning. Sometimes I took public transportation, which I had never done before. I altered my lunch time and I tried different restaurants and varied menus. I also changed some of my work routines. I switched a regular afternoon meeting to the morning, and I cut out other meetings altogether. These changes definitely enhanced my awareness level. Generally, I became conscious of spending more one-on-one time with my staff people. The thought of being a "gardener of potential" appealed to me.

At home I consciously made an effort to "afflict" my comfortable ways by breaking some of the patterns I had become accustomed to. I changed our menu for greater variety, took a more active interest in the children's schoolwork, planned some different family activities that focused on fun, and even shot some hoops with my son. I noticed an increase in energy as I shifted out of a habit pattern. Aware of all the new possibilities open to me, I felt totally alert. I had seldom felt this way before, and I realized it was because my old habit pattern had obscured my perception. I knew how blinded I had become. How subtle those habit loops are, I thought to myself. Not knowing we're in the loops, we can't see our way out.

I now realized that the Wizard was right. The mind needs to be jarred out of its natural complacency. There is, however, dislocation and discontinuity before new routines can be established. But I was discovering that this discontinuity offered me the rich potential of creativity. I could fill that new void with anything I wished. Any number of possibilities existed. This awareness also gave me a renewed appreciation of the time-saving efficiency of a good routine.

All in all, my discoveries were an innervating experience, and I felt a new flush of aliveness. I could feel an urgency in my work, and I wanted to know how this urgency differed from importance, as the Wizard had suggested.

When we met again, the Wizard was in his garden. A month had passed and it was now late summer. I shared my excitement with him, especially about the increased level of awareness I experienced when I started new routines.

"Congratulations!" he said. "It takes courage to do what you did, and commitment. If you had been unwilling to try something different, you never would have felt that aliveness that comes from breaking new ground." With that, the Wizard made a sweeping gesture over a plowed portion of his garden plot.

"What you discovered was the challenge and excitement of open space, that time between the end of the old and the beginning of the new. Open space is a seedbed for creativity. We cannot be creative while locked into habit patterns. Breaking the habit enables us to fill the void with new initiatives. To gain control of our lives we have to relinquish control. It is one of life's great paradoxes."

"It sounds like double-talk to me," I said skeptically.

"On the contrary. It is really quite logical. In order to gain control of any situation with a new initiative, we have to surrender control of the old. This death of the old and birth of the new is the cycle of creation that creates open space in the interim. Traditional managers are not comfortable with open space. To them, unstructured time is unproductive time. They like to fill each moment with planned efforts. This, however, does not allow for the creative process to take place. Open space is essential for radical change."

"Radical change?" I struggled to mask my surprise.

The Wizard reached down and pulled out some large weeds from between the tomato plants. Working the roots free of the warm, moist soil, the Wizard held the fragile tendrils in his fingers.

"*Radical* is from the Latin word meaning "root," so I am talking about change at the roots. If I tear out these tomatoes and then plant corn, that is a radical change. Radical change requires open space. To do that I have to 'let go' of my tomatoes and create an open space in which to sow my seed corn. It is the open space that makes the planting of seed corn possible."

I played back my understanding: "You're saying that open space is the fertile soil of change, and if I program my life too tightly, I will lose the potential for new directions in my life."

"You said it well," encouraged the Wizard. "Children need unstructured time to nurture their imagination and creative potential. This is the purpose of play. For adults, unstructured open space is our playtime. It is like open soil, and it provides the potential for radical change. As long as we have open space, we have potential in our lives. We can fill the space with any creative idea we choose. Once we fill that space, however, we commit ourselves to a new initiative which, like the corn, takes root as a new idea, a different routine."

"And once the new idea takes root, it's here to stay until we uproot it for something else. Right?" I asked. "Is change always a radical, uprooting process?"

"No, only radical change is uprooting. As long as we are committed to a new idea, we do not uproot it. We nurture it. This is what I did with the tomatoes a moment ago. I made it easier for them to grow by removing the weeds, not the tomatoes. This is change of a more gradual, incremental kind that supports and nurtures the existing idea; whereas radical change pulls up the idea by its roots and replaces it with another. The optimal time to make significant change is when things are unsettled, like an unplanted garden. That is the fluid state of open space, the time to sow the seeds of our choice."

"The change may have been gradual for the tomatoes, but it was radical for the weeds!" I quipped with a mischievous smile.

The Wizard smiled back, enjoying my emerging playful manner. "Gradual change is the kind we make to improve an existing idea. For this process, we need a certain order and stability. The existing idea, pattern, or procedure in our lives provides this. But when the pattern breaks down, as it inevitably will, chaos and confusion set in. This is open space, the seedbed for radical change—the rich soil where a new pattern will grow. Innovative leaders in the business community who understand this concept always use the uncertainty of chaos to make changes. Those who do not understand this process tend to impose controls that strangle the nascent change process."

"So we go from order to chaos and then back to order again," I summarized.

"That is exactly right. There is a time to pull up the weeds around the plants, and a time to pull up the plants themselves. Knowing when to do one or the other is an art."

"Some controlling managers do this to people," said the Wizard reaching down and unceremoniously yanking a premature carrot out of the ground. He scrutinized it with mock serious intent, then smiled as he handed it to me saying, "In doing this, they destroy what they seek to gain. Tagore, the great Indian poet said, 'Emancipation from the bondage of the soil is no freedom for the tree.'"

"Or for the carrot," I smiled, knowingly. "I can identify with that. I've had that done to me."

"Yes," concluded the Wizard, "the chaos and uncertainty of open space offers the possibility of something new. Once we initiate the new, we enter a period of stability where we refine and improve our new order. In time, as this pattern ages and becomes increasingly less effective, we feel the need for radical change again. And so the cycle continues."

"Speaking of cycle," I said, looking down at the barren patches in his garden, "it looks as if you have reaped some of the fruits of your labor here. Are you enjoying the harvest?"

"Yes, thank you, I am. Nature continues to bless me with more abundance than usual. I am counting on a longer growing season than usual."

"Then your chores weren't as urgent as you expected."

"We must learn to create our own urgency on matters of importance. If we wait for situations to become urgent, we lose control of the situation and we eventually lose control of our lives. That is why we must take immediate action on things that are very important, even on those things that do not appear to be urgent."

The Wizard had planted this idea with me during our last meeting. It was now time for it to germinate. "Wizard, are you saying urgent is not important?"

"That is right. In fact, you could say they are opposites."

"That is hard for me to imagine," I said skeptically, folding my arms in a "prove-it-to-me" posture.

The Wizard smoothed out the fine topsoil in an open corner of his garden. He then took a stick and drew a line to form two columns. At the top of one he scratched a big "U" for Urgent, and in the other column he scratched a big "I" for Important.

"The distinction we make here will help you break the habit that everything is urgent. We will define *urgent* as immediate, a short-term crisis or problem. Whereas, *important* is significant, something that could really make a difference, a long term opportunity or possibility."

Then the Wizard roughly scratched several words under the two letters:

U	I
immediate	significant
short-term	long-term
crisis/problem	opportunity/possibility

"In day-to-day life, the urgent and the routine drive out the important. After taking care of the routine and urgent matters, typically no time is left for the important. This is the problem with crisis management. It can only get us back to where we were before the crisis started. It does not move us forward. When we become exclusively problem solvers, we allow the urgency of events to dictate our priorities. We become consumed with crises, trampled by the march of events. In the words of one executive, we become 'fodder for time.' "

"You've just described my life," I admitted.

"The reason for this is simple," said the Wizard. "Problems are pushy. They are very aggressive, forcing themselves upon us. Possibilities are shy, and they must be sought out. It is like having two employees or two children—one named 'Problem' and the other 'Possibility.' The one is always intruding in our lives; the other is reticent, unobtrusive, scarcely noticed. Who takes up most of our time?"

"Problem," I answered, nodding my head knowingly.

"Imagine that you are at the office working with Peter Problem. He is taking up all of your time. Standing outside your door, unnoticed, is Paula Possibility, too shy to come in. Paula is patient, like all possibilities, waiting to be invited in. But nothing happens because of your preoccupation with Peter. Now Paula faces a choice. One option is to slip silently away, as most possibilities do. You as a manager will not be accountable for this unknown lost opportunity. But Paula can also lose her patience, burst into your office, and demand to be heard. In choosing this option, however, she is no longer a possibility. She is now Paula Problem, and her message is urgent. Now we have two problems, Peter and Paula. And, unlike possibilities, you will be held accountable for solving both of them."

"Paula Problem is like a phone ringing or a baby crying. Somebody has to pick it up." I could identify with this situation.

"That is right," acknowledged the Wizard, "but managers have become so enamored of problem solving that they have lost sight of possibilities. If your focus is only on problem solving, you will find yourself at the end of the year wondering where the time went and what you really have accomplished. Now you are a year older, more distressed, and you have little of substance to show for the time you have spent. Life has been a rescue and salvage operation, exhilarating at times, but ultimately exhausting. This is the road to professional and personal burnout."

"I can speak to that," I said, my shoulders sagging under a heavy weight. "So what can I do?"

"Become more creative," said the Wizard. "Only through a creative search for possibilities can you run your business without it running you! You can no longer be just a problem solver. You must also become a possibility seeker. Some people, of course, will always see problems. Significantly fewer will see the ever-present possibilities in all situations. The difference here is in attitude and perception, in how you look at life."

"I'm sure that's true, but why is it so?"

"I believe it has to do with the immediacy of problems. Problems are usually 'in-your-face' phenomena."

Intrigued, I asked, "When does a possibility become a problem?"

"For a possibility seeker, it never really does. If a problem is not picked up early, it simply presents itself as a 'late possibility.' It is an eleventh hour opportunity to do something that should have been done sooner."

"Aren't you just playing with words when you call a problem a late possibility?"

"It is much more than that," explained the Wizard. "Problem solving can only put us back on track, continuing where we left off; but what if we are on the wrong track? A 'late possibility' tells us we may still have time to lay some new track. If we sense these possibilities, problems provide us with the opportunity to lift ourselves to a new level beyond where we left off. Every crisis is an opportunity. Every illness is a chance to be stronger and healthier than before. We have the capacity to position ourselves better for tomorrow as a result of every experience we face today, especially the bad ones."

"It's all in how you see things, isn't it?" I said. "It's the difference between getting back to normal versus being better than before. Normal could be getting back into the old rut again, couldn't it? So I can use any problem as a means or an opportunity to get me out of a rut, beyond where I am."

I could tell from the Wizard's words he was pleased with my response. "It is all a matter of perception, as you said. Solving problems only restores us to our former ways. Possibilities, however, have the power to change our ways. They arouse us, uplift us, and offer hope. The power of possibilities is their ability to sustain us through the problems we face."

"The key is to keep our problems in perspective, right?"

"Yes, keep them in the context of possibilities. Without possibilities, problems can be overpowering. And some problems will even diminish as you pursue possibilities. When you are working on the important things in your life, fewer crises will develop.

"Remember purpose? Purpose empowers possibilities and overpowers problems. In time you will gain control over the fragmented parts of your life and have more time to do the things you want to do."

"It makes so much sense. Why don't we do it more often?" I wondered.

"I will let you in on a secret," whispered the Wizard, drawing me closer. "We do not want to admit it but, in truth, most of us like things the way they are. Crises make the big decisions for us. They get the energy flowing and dictate where the time and attention go. Like autocratic managers or dictatorial parents, problems tell us what to do. In doing so, they spare us the difficulty of making tough choices."

"So letting problems set our priorities is a lazy way of running a business, or a life. It's a cop-out."

"That is exactly right. Chasing after problems is an easy way you can avoid some difficult existential questions and some fundamental management decisions."

"So then what do I do?" I thought I knew the answer but I wanted to hear it from the Wizard.

"So what do you do about the problems in your life? Try

something simple—create a 'possibility crisis!' Converting a possibility into a crisis is like inducing labor. You can precipitate a 'possibility crisis' on your own terms before a possibility goes away or becomes a problem. This is the only way a possibility can hope to compete with the immediacy of a crisis. You have to make the possibility more tangible and appealing, more exciting to attract the energies of those you wish to involve.

"The idea is to get people excited about a possibility and then to determine what must be done *now* if it is to become a reality. Then you take that first step with the same urgency that you address any crisis. That is a 'possibility crisis.' If it is not done now, we may lose the opportunity. That is what leadership is all about. Leaders are possibility precipitators. They empower us with the immediate presence of possibilities."

"What about managers?" I asked entreatingly.

"Oh, they are definitely more problem solvers than possibility precipitators."

"That's fascinating! Clearly, I've been more a manager than a leader. You're saying I should take the initiative by precipitating a possibility crisis of my own choice rather than responding to problems that force themselves upon me."

"It is not a case of either/or." The Wizard was not limited to either/or thinking. "You will have to deal with both problems and possibilities, but it is a matter of balancing your priorities. Precipitating possibility crises is a must, or you will never get long-term control over your life. When you are working within the realm of possibilities, you must deal with crises as they come. Problems are subordinated to the possibilities and, in time, they will diminish in number and intensity. This is how you can gain mastery over your work life. You must both lead and manage."

"I see I have a lot more to learn about this," I said, shaking my head.

"Only by focusing on possibilities can you break out of the gravitational pull of your problems. You have to think about potential to get beyond the present problems. Possibilities lurk in open space and offer the potential for quantum change."

"I'd really like to know more about how to find these possibilities."

As he had in our past meetings, the Wizard prepared me for the next stage. "It all begins with the images you carry around in your mind. These imaginative internal pictures usually dominate the images you receive from the outside world. A clear mental image of a desirable possibility is a compelling thing. If you desire something and visualize it very clearly, it is likely to happen. That is why it is very important to be aware of what is on your mind. We will talk about that another time if you wish to arrange another meeting, but right now my rose bushes need attention. I can see their possibilities, but if I wait much longer, I could have a problem on my hands."

The Wizard caressed the fragile blooms of his rose bushes. "The growing season is short in the Midwest, far too short. I do not like to see it come to an end, for these flowers give me so much joy. I know that if I take some action now, I will experience their floral abundance again in the next year. That is the way life is."

Suggestions

The Wizard felt the following suggestions could really make a difference in my life.

- Make a list of things you would like to do that could really make a difference in your job. Assume that all the things you are now doing are routine or problem-oriented issues. Make this your list of exciting, new, and fun possibilities— things you have a passion for.
- Ask yourself which of the items on your list could have a significant long-term impact on your business operation.

Select one of the possibilities from each list. Break it down into steps and number them in sequence. Then, make the first step a "possibility crisis" and do it now. Take real action and follow through with each new step. Here is an example:

Item

Spend more one-on-one time with my colleagues.

Steps

1. Development of people is a manager's first responsibility, and the vehicle to do this is the work itself.
2. With Dick Leider's wise aphorism (*Repacking Your Bags*) in mind—"Live passionately for today and purposefully for tomorrow"—ask each person what commitment she/he would *like* to consider that would make a significant difference. (To make the company more customer-focused or whatever your thrust may be.)
3. This commitment must be something that they feel is meaningful (purposeful) for them and the company, something that they feel strongly (passionately) about, and something they are willing to take personal responsibility for.
4. Have them then develop an action plan with specific steps, dates, and times, to get it started.
5. Create an entrepreneurial climate by removing obstacles, real or imagined, and helping them to connect with resources they may need. The object is for them to *feel* empowered. Remember, this is something they *want* to do, so the responsibility for keeping you informed is on them.

Step back and watch the energy release!

Do it now!

Make it happen!

Get on with it!

6
The Power of Possibilities

Ultimately, leaders do not possess visions;
visions possess leaders.

I **began** to find immediate applications in my life for the distinction between what is urgent and what is important. I discovered that 95% of my time was spent in routine and urgent activities, like responding to demands imposed upon me by others at work, and putting out "fires" that might have been easily prevented. At home I found I spent much time monitoring disputes between my children. The Wizard was right. There was no time for the important things in my life. In the month that followed our last meeting, I discontinued several activities, I delegated others, and I continually asked myself the question; "Is what I'm doing the best use of my time right now?"

I witnessed the empowering nature of possibilities as I counseled my staff on what they could do to impact our company in a significant way. An entrepreneurial spirit began to bloom as the important issues were being addressed and people began to feel they could "make a difference." In less than a month I had transformed the way I managed my business. The Wizard had predicted that this one change of perception would change my work habits significantly. Nothing I did on the job before had so dramatically changed things as this. I was also seeing positive changes in my family life as I changed my focus from problems to possibilities. In my excitement, I called the Wizard and asked if I could see him the following day. When I arrived, I found the Wizard sitting on his front porch.

"I'm so pleased I was able to see you on such short notice," I told him. "I didn't think you'd be available."

"I purposely keep open space on my calendar," replied the Wizard. "If you recall, that is fertile time. When I allow my day to be cluttered with busywork, I have no time for creative possibilities, and no time for you."

"Is helping me what you consider important?" I inquired timidly.

"Is it important to you?"

"Why, yes. Of course it is."

"Then it is important to me," said the Wizard. "Tell me, what have you discovered since we last met?"

"I discovered that I wasn't doing anything really important, so I had a team-building session with my subordinates, and we came up with a vision for our company." I spoke with pride. "We're now working on a set of objectives to carry it out. I can see a difference already."

"I am not surprised," rejoined the Wizard. "I would suggest, however, that you not use the word *subordinate*. We have talked about the powerful effect language has on us. If you label people as subordinate, they will become so. You want to empower them, not subordinate them. It is a useful word in the military, but is has no place in our vocabulary today."

"What do you suggest?" I asked, a bit surprised.

"Anything that does not limit them—people, colleagues, members, associates, partners, affiliates, staff, delegates. . . ." The Wizard raised his eyebrows and opened his palms as if to offer me my choice.

"They don't sound the same," I said.

"They are not the same. We are talking about a change of perception, and language can help us make that change. You will get used to using them, like using the word *vision*. Not long ago, vision was taboo in business. Now it is fashionable.

Times change, and words change to reflect the times." said the Wizard.

"I guess you're right." I said. "Then the word *superior* is out, too?"

"Absolutely," the Wizard replied unequivocally. "That is a dreadful word! When the industrial revolution began and people flocked to the cities to work in factories, employers faced the problem of managing large numbers of people. The only model they had for management was the military, so they adopted its methods and its language. The military model outlived its usefulness long ago, but the methods and the language persist. Changing the language will help us change our methods."

"What model do we have to take its place?" I asked.

"That is the question," affirmed the Wizard. "We are in a transitional period where the old no longer works and the new is unfamiliar and ill-defined. I suspect there will be a variety of models to replace the old one. The terms *superior* and *subordinate* indicate a rigid structural order. The old pyramid with its hierarchy of boxes, levels, and channels of communication is just too inflexible."

"But you have to have *some* structure." I was struggling with the possibilities here.

The Wizard placed his feet squarely on the porch floor and firmly gripped the arms of his rocker. Holding them for a moment, he then reached out with his knuckles and rapped sharply on the pillar beside him, as if to test its soundness. "To be sure, structure is vital, but it must serve us and not get in the way. Networks of individuals and teams are replacing the pyramid as the most effective means of communication. The CEO of the General Electric Company says his objective is to create a 'boundaryless company.' "

"How do you control employees with a network or without boundaries?" I was genuinely puzzled.

"You do not control, nor do you want to. The *release* of energy, rather than its control, is the emphasis you want. In the information age, we have to access data quickly. Power lies in sharing, not withholding information. Leaders have a vision of what they want to accomplish, and the people throughout the network feel empowered to make it happen. This provides a looser but more powerful form of control. Visions do not fit neatly into a tightly-controlled organization."

For me the questions were coming faster than the answers. "How's that?" I asked.

"Visions are commitments to the self to make something happen, but they cross functional boundaries, go well beyond job descriptions, and often exceed the authority given to the job. As such," said the Wizard, "traditional structures cannot cope with visions."

"So what can I do, Wizard, to change the structure of my business?"

"We need more fluid organizations and more open space so people can get on with their commitments. Networks of people creatively interacting serve this purpose perfectly. In organizations that encourage this, people find support they never knew existed. The organizational synergy is enormous."

My orderly world was crumbling all around me. I responded in the only way I knew. "It sounds chaotic."

"It is, and that is good. Creativity is chaotic. It is never neat and orderly. Have you ever visited an artist's studio? It is a disaster! Paint is everywhere. Some of it, the relevant colors and amounts, finds its way to the canvas, and somehow it all comes together. To the artist, the vision on her mind is as clear as the finished painting, but the open space between the image and the finished product is rather messy. The same is true for any creative endeavor. In business, however, it is not paint but ideas, energy, and information that is living and chaotic. Controlling that is like telling the artist what and how to paint."

As always, the Wizard was convincing. "That's a good analogy. You've made a strong point for vision. That's why I had that session with my subord— . . . with my *staff*," I said, correcting myself. "I am not sure, however, that I fully grasp the concept of vision. Could you help me understand it better?"

"I would be happy to. *Vision* is such a misunderstood word.

First of all, it is not something 'out there' in the future." The Wizard pointed across the road, out past the dry corn stalks in a field, out to the horizon. Then, putting his finger to his head, he added, "It is in here, and it is happening now. It is a here-and-now, not a there-and-then, phenomenon. Vision is a living thing, and the more we think about it, the more it grows in clarity and intensity. This is what makes a leader powerful—the capacity to envision a desired state and to communicate it in a clear and compelling manner. Ultimately, leaders do not possess visions; visions possess leaders. This is how leaders make things happen."

The Wizard could not conceal an impish look. "It has been said that there are three kinds of people—those who make things happen, those who watch things happen, and those who do not know what happened!"

I laughed. "I regret that I am probably one of those people who don't know what's happened."

"And you are not alone," encouraged the Wizard. "The art lies in seeing possibilities, in seeing what you want. When you visualize something, you see it in your mind's eye. You don't know where this is except that it lies beyond what you can literally see. As such, seeing possibilities is beyond the limitation of our senses. That is the power of imagination. You can imagine what you wish, unencumbered by conscious constraints. You can transcend your problems and soar into the realm of pure possibilities."

My face lit up. "I just made a connection. In our last meeting, we talked about being possibility seekers. Imagination is the means by which we do so."

"You have just answered your own question, How do I become a possibility seeker?" said the Wizard. "You decide what you want, and then you imagine it to be so. You can become a possibility seeker by seeing the possibility in your mind's eye. Imagination makes the future happen now. Remember too, you energize the image by the act of imagining it. In other words, just thinking about it makes it more likely to happen. Focusing your mind empowers the object of your focus. This is the strength of concentration."

The Wizard began to pace back and forth with excitement. "A vision is a creative act. You have brought something into being. The artist has an image of what she wants to create before painting it on canvas, and the writer sees the plot unfolding in his mind before putting it on paper. This is the initial step in a sequence that translates image into reality. Vision is the start of a mysterious process that transforms dreams into reality. It is the link between mind and body, the first step in an action sequence powered by feelings."

"Powered by feelings?"

"Feelings empower," said the Wizard. "If you reflect on an event of the past, the feelings associated with that event come with it. Try it. Think back to a particularly satisfying moment in your life."

I remained silent for a moment, and then I slowly started to smile.

"You are enjoying yourself," observed the Wizard.

"I was thinking about when my son was born. That was the happiest moment in my life. I had always wanted a boy. While I was thinking about that event, I could actually feel some of the same sensations I experienced sixteen years ago." I cocked my head to one side in a reflective trance, glowing in silent remembrance.

The Wizard softly said, "You've made my point."

I looked up at the Wizard, and he continued. "A mental image of a past event summons the feelings that accompany it, as you have just demonstrated. Now remember this: The same is true when you project an image forward. For example, if you wish to be a more loving person, you simply have to imagine yourself so, and you will begin to feel more loving. The feelings will empower you to act towards others and towards yourself in a more loving manner. This may surprise you, but the mind does not know the difference between a vivid mental image and the real thing, something concrete and already manifested in your life."

"Wizard, are you saying that something in my head is the same as the real thing? I find that very hard to believe," I said skeptically.

"If the image is vivid enough, then as far as your mind is concerned, it is the same as physical reality. Tell me, when you see an attractive person on the street, does that person do something to you emotionally and physically?" asked the Wizard, zeroing in on my skepticism.

"Of course," I responded quickly. I didn't want to give the Wizard the impression that I was emotionally inert.

"Good. Now then, close your eyes and visualize that attractive person who stirs you emotionally. See yourself interacting together in a pleasurable setting. Feel the energy present—intellectual, physical, emotional. Observe the subtle ways that you find so attractive—the warm and affectionate eyes, the way the other person laughs, the spontaneity and natural manner. Notice how responsive that person is to your every movement. Savor the intimacy of the moment, just the two of you. Feel the . . ."

"Stop!" I said playfully. "I get the point. You had me in another world."

"On the contrary," said the Wizard, "you had yourself in another world!"

"Okay, I'm sold. Now tell me how I can use this wonderful visualizing power."

The Wizard stood up and walked into the house. A moment later he returned with a book of writings by Thomas Carlyle, the brilliant nineteenth-century Scottish historian. The Wizard quoted Carlyle: "The thought is always the ancestor of the deed." Allowing a moment for the thought to sink in, he continued, "You recall when we recently met, we talked about perception and action. What you view or what you see in your mind determines what you do."

"But, Wizard, you also said the process works the other way as well. What I do effects the way I view things," I challenged.

"Yes, that is exactly right. Your experience will determine what you see and how you see it. That completes the loop—what you see determines what you do, and what you do determines what you see. You now go around in that loop, repeating your behavior mindlessly. If you wish to change your behavior, you have to change the images in your mind. It is simply a matter of choice, replacing the old image with a new one. The thought is always the ancestor of the deed. If you want to change your deeds, you have to change its ancestors, which are your thoughts."

"Is a change in thought really the only way out?"

"It is the only permanent way out," said the Wizard. "You can break the cycle with a simple change of behavior, but it will be short-lived if the mental image does not change with it. Remember, it is the image you carry in your mind that tends to prevail over the images coming from the outside. You see the world from the inside out. These mindsets, the habitual patterns you have set for yourself, are difficult to break."

Repeating the Wizard's words from an earlier time, I said, "That is why we need to 'afflict the comfortable,' by jarring our perception."

"You remember well. Einstein said that we determine reality by the 'kingdom within us.' That is why it is important to know your inner orientations. Many of us are programmed with beliefs and mindsets that prevent us from making new choices and creatively interacting with others. Some of these patterns date back to our childhood. The good news is that you have a choice. You can reprogram yourself. Anything that has been programmed into us can be deprogrammed out of us. There is a simple way, but it will have to wait. In the meantime, if you practice visualization, you will not be disappointed. That is the way life is."

Suggestions

The thought is always ancestor of the deed. The Wizard said to start with these visualization exercises, and I'd begin to see some changes.

- Hold something in front of you. Look at the object carefully. Then close your eyes, and see if you can re-create it in your mind's eye. Practice closing your eyes and visualizing things not in front of you.

- Close your eyes and follow the same mind's eye re-creation process for sounds, smells, tastes, and touch. Notice whether you can re-create all the senses equally well. Which is your dominant sense? The visual sense is dominant for most of us. Work with your less dominant senses as well as your dominant one to broaden your range of imaging.

- Close your eyes, and see yourself doing something that you really want to do. See yourself doing it perfectly. If you have difficulty seeing yourself doing it, visualize someone who does it well. Then replace that image with yourself. When you can see yourself doing this and you can feel the pull toward doing it, you may begin physically to take the steps to make it happen.

- Visualize a project in its completed state. See it now in your mind's eye as you would like it to be. Feel the satisfaction of its completion and feel the desirability of its accomplishment. Repeat the visualization and feeling process as often as you wish. Savor the joy of this possibility. Allow the good feelings of this image to motivate you to act on it. Keep the vision clearly in mind to carry you through any obstacle you might encounter.

Believe in the possibility!

7

Imagination— The New Reality

The truth is that you energize what you think about. You empower what you attend to.

For the next several weeks I was obsessed with my new insights on vision. To me, vision had only been a fancy word for long-range planning, like setting management objectives at work. Vision was always dressed up a little bit so it could be framed and hung on the walls as executive boilerplate— something that nobody could disagree with, nor get excited about.

Now vision had become a living thing. I vividly recalled how the Wizard had demonstrated through mental imagery that the mind and the body are one. The link between thoughts and feelings is very real in the recollection of past events. This certainly was not a new idea, but somehow I had never realized how it could be consciously applied to my future. I saw the possibilities of the future and the present becoming one with imagination. I was practicing pure alchemy, transmuting baser metals into gold!

I was also eager to see the Wizard again and learn the simple way to visualize and change mindsets. When the Wizard and I met again, he invited me to take a walk behind his house. We strolled through a wooded area of maple, oak, birch, aspen, and Norway pine. We walked silently for some minutes when the Wizard paused and, seeing a fallen birch, peeled off a small strip of its white outer bark. Taking a pen from his pocket, he drew a circle on the birch bark.

"You will recall the habit loop, the mindset, that began with perception—what you see determines what you do." He wrote the word *Image* at the top of his circle. "All perception is imagery, mental imagery. Everything you see is an image in your brain. In that sense, all reality is imagery to you."

"You're saying it all starts with imagery," I repeated.

"Yes," said the Wizard as he moved his pen clockwise on the circle, writing the words *Feeling* and *Action* to form a three-step process. "The image is the key because it evokes the behavioral process that follows—an image arouses feelings, feelings precipitate action, and action reinforces the image.

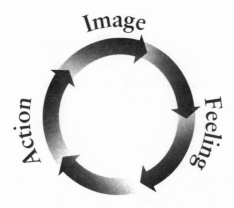

"All conscious acts begin with an image. Feeling and action convert that image into reality. And a vision is an image in here." The Wizard pointed to his head.

"Having the vision inside you links your future with your present. When you visualize something, it becomes real to your mind—now. In other words, in your mind's eye it is actually happening. In effect, you have fooled the mind into thinking it is occurring because it does not know the difference between vivid imagery and the actual happening. Once your mind grasps that desirable vision and actually sees it happening, it is hard for it to let go. That vision creates compelling commitment, and you find yourself drawn inexorably toward the new reality in your mind. It is powerful stuff."

"I see what you mean," I said. "You're getting excited just talking about it."

The Wizard excitedly continued. "Have you ever imagined something and said, 'It was so real I could see it happening'? Vivid mental imagery employs all the senses. This reveals another secret: Thinking about possibilities generates more excitement than thinking about problems. The energizing nature of possibilities enables you to surmount your problems. Without a vision, your problems can become overwhelming. With a vision, your problems become merely nettlesome obstacles. The Book of Proverbs says, 'Where there is no vision, the people perish.' The same could be said of today's business."

"Aren't you just talking about visionary leaders, charismatic types—the few that have this talent?" I asked.

"Surely this gift is well developed in extraordinary business leaders, but all of us have this capability. You may recall I said that belief in another's potential is an empowering act. When you believe in people, you will help them become more responsible for themselves. They will feel encouraged to take charge of their own lives and rise above the problems they face. It is true for associates at work. It is also true for people in personal relationships with you, from significant others to children. This is the message in *The Wizard of Oz*. The Tin Man, the Scarecrow, and the Cowardly Lion all felt empowered with the gifts they received: a heart, a brain, and courage.

"The sporting world is filled with stories of coaches who empowered doubting athletes to reach performance potentials previously unknown to them. The same is true in the world of medicine. Doctors often encourage patients to use the formidable powers of their minds to rise above their afflictions."

"So why should we expect less from the business world?" I asked.

"Exactly. A friend of mine wanted to remodel his house. Four builders were asked to bid. Three saw nothing but problems. The fourth laid out several exciting possibilities. When my friend asked him how he was able to come up with so many ideas, he replied, 'I see beyond the walls.' Asked what he meant by that statement, the builder pointed outside to some shrubbery obscured by a wall of the house. 'Those bushes are too lovely to sit out there unseen. I imagine how they would look from your living room, without the walls. I see beyond the walls.'

"With mental imagery, you can see 'beyond the walls' to the possibilities that lie ahead. You can break out of what William Blake called your 'mind-forged manacles' and see the possibilities unfold before you."

"Very interesting," I said. "I'm beginning to see some connections. Last time we met, you asked me to become a 'possibility seeker.' Now you're saying that mental imagery and feelings convert these possibilities into action. This three-step process takes us 'beyond the walls' imposed by problems. Presumably the vision is attractive enough to carry us through the problems. Without the vision, we could lose the will to continue. Right?"

Looking rather pleased, the Wizard smiled. "I could not have said it better. Mental imagery brings the future to life within you right now. This starts a process that translates the image into reality. When an image in your mind becomes real to you, it becomes your 'new reality.' You have seen something better and you are no longer satisfied with the old reality, the way things are. It is this dynamic that literally lifts you out of the comfort zone of the old way, pulling you into the new reality of possibilities. Pierre Currie said, 'It is necessary to make life a dream, and of that dream, a reality.' That says it all."

"The future becomes the present by my ability to imagine something as if it were so," I echoed. "But surely you're not saying that all I have to do to make something happen is to just see it in my mind's eye."

"Of course not. But this is the first step, and without taking it, it is very unlikely that anything will happen. The truth is that you energize what you think about. You empower what you attend to. Action follows mental imagery. And when you use your imagination, you receive a very special bonus."

"What's that?"

"Imagery activates the right hemisphere of the brain, which is closely linked with the unconscious mind. With the image clearly and vividly in mind, you can program the unconscious to help you attain what you have in mind. This is an awesome force to have as an ally. The unconscious is where habits are stored. Through imagery you literally reprogram your unconscious mind with new habits to help you get what you want. Things that people attribute to luck, good fortune, coincidence, or synchronicity are often the work of the unconscious mind selecting and screening inputs to the conscious mind."

"I think I know what you mean," I said hesitantly. "A friend of mine is a naturalist. He finds wildlife where no one else can, probably because he has conditioned his mind to seek it out. Nature's clues are there for all to see, but they are noticed only by those whose minds are trained to see them."

The Wizard reached down beside the path. Brushing aside the larger fronds of an ostrich fern, he found a wild raspberry bush sheltered beneath it. Gently he removed a berry and handed it to me.

"How did you know it was there?" I asked.

"Just as you said before, I have trained myself to see these things."

"I remember the first time I bought tires for my car," I reminisced. "I thought I was lucky to find an ad for tires on sale. Later, I realized tires are always on sale. I just had never noticed the ads until I needed tires."

"Need has a wonderful way of focusing the mind."

"I know what you mean. Last year, I had to give a talk on a subject I knew little about. In preparing for it, information came to me from sources I never expected. At the time, I thought it was a remarkable coincidence. In hindsight, I can now see how the unconscious mind alerted me to images that would normally have gone unnoticed."

"Yes, mental imagery, with the help of a trained unconscious mind, gets you 'beyond the walls' of your limiting or negative mindsets."

"If I think of negative things, do I strengthen them as well?" I wondered.

"To be sure," replied the Wizard. "The negative things in your life are the walls. You can redirect negativity with positive imagery." With that, the Wizard stopped on the wooded pathway. He turned toward me with the birch bark still in his hand, and he wrote the word *negative* in front of each of the three words on the circle: *Negative* Image, *Negative* Feeling, *Negative* Action.

"You may recall a few sessions ago we talked about distress and stage fright. If you do not see yourself as capable of giving a speech, then the mere thought of it terrifies you. It raises your stress level and floods you with feelings of fear and inadequacy, making it nearly impossible for you to speak effectively. Some say that in our society giving a speech is the number one fear, death being farther down on the list. People would rather die than give a speech!"

I laughed. "I know. I can identify with that."

"Well, you can conquer stage fright in a simple way. The cycle can be broken at two places." Again, the Wizard pointed to the circle he had drawn on the bark, and he scratched out the word *negative*. "First, break the cycle at the image stage simply by redirecting your energy from worrying to a positive image. All you have to do is to see yourself performing successfully. See the audience responding positively and feel the euphoria of the moment. Imagine the people coming up to you afterwards and saying how much they enjoyed your talk. This will arrest the worry and start the energy moving toward a positive experience."

With that, the Wizard scratched off the remaining two negatives and said, "Positive mental imagery transforms and redirects negative energy."

Having had some unpleasant speaking experiences, I was still doubtful. "I find it hard to believe it's that easy."

"I never said it was easy. The process is simple, but simple is seldom easy." The Wizard had repeatedly made this point. "Even the doubts you express now will erode the process. The image in your mind of a speech with a wonderful outcome must be very desirable, very compelling. Then it will begin to unfold."

"You said there were two places where the negative cycle could be broken," I reminded the Wizard.

"Yes. The second place to break the negative cycle is at the action stage. You give a great speech simply by acting 'as if' you were a great speaker. In California, they say you 'fake it 'til you make it.' It is a well-known acting principle. The late Cary Grant, perhaps the most loved actor of his time, said he was successful because he pretended to be someone he wanted to be until he became that person. Act and you shall become. What you are really doing is selling yourself."

"Selling myself?"

"Effective salespeople do not sell products, they help the buyer imagine satisfaction. People buy products that they imagine will make them more comfortable, more secure, more desirable, more confident—whatever they would like themselves to be. When they link this image in their minds to the product, they buy. Technically speaking, they sell themselves.

"The process of creating mental imagery is a buying cycle. When you imagine something you want, you are 'buying in' to a new image, an image of a better you, a better life, or a better world. After creating these images of satisfaction, the salesperson then acts 'as if' the other has bought. This positive expectation contributes to a positive outcome. When you do not have a salesperson to help you imagine, you can go through the process yourself. That's why I say that creating mental imagery is really selling yourself. It is a time-tested process."

I realized that what the Wizard was talking about had just happened to me. I had just 'bought in.' "It's really pretty simple, isn't it? Do you have any suggestions on how I can start the whole process?"

"An easy way to begin," said the Wizard, "is with affirmations. An affirmation is simply a statement you make to yourself that affirms the image in your mind. With affirmations, you can talk to yourself using words to describe the image. This 'self-talk' affirms the future outcome, as if it were already so. Positive mental imagery and affirmations are powerful forces for change. Images activate the right hemisphere of the brain. Affirmations activate the left, or language side. Together, images and affirmations enlist the powers of the whole brain."

"So what I say to myself is just as important as what I image," I said.

"The outcome is best when they work together. Often, however, your self-talk is negative and works against the positive imagery, or your talk is positive but you cannot see anything good happening. Positive self-talk is needed to affirm the imagination, to put the image into words. For example, if you wish to be more assertive, you simply state the affirmation as if it were so, and you visualize it simultaneously: 'I am an assertive person,' or 'People appreciate my assertive manner.'

"Affirmations are short, specific, positive, and always in the present tense. Simply say as you see it. Your purpose in using them is to offset everything negative and to embed in your mind the positive image you wish to create. When the image becomes vividly clear and compellingly desirable, then you will be moved to take action. You will have empowered an image and brought it into being. That is action a manager can understand," he said, smiling at me. "Speaking of action, are you an aerobic-walker?"

"I'm not sure what you mean by that." I was a bit fearful of what I might be asked to do.

"Right now, I feel the need to quicken the pace, to raise my heart rate a bit. When I do this, I imagine I am a world-class walker. Come with me, and I will show you how to do it." With that, the Wizard set out briskly on the path. Looking back over his shoulder he smiled and, bending his arms at the elbows, began pumping them vigorously and forged ahead with a sudden burst of speed.

Suggestions

The Wizard had me combine positive affirmations with mental imagery. The following guidelines were useful as I prepared my own affirmations:

- Create as many affirmations as you wish. Begin with one to start the process.
- Write the affirmation down and repeat it as often as you wish.
- The best times to concentrate on your affirmation are in moments of relaxed awareness, during quiet times of reflection.
- When repeating your affirmation, reflect on its meaning and experience the feelings it induces. Visualize yourself experiencing the desired state.
- Remove all doubt in your mind.
- Spend as much time on your affirmation as your concentration allows. A few moments may be ample.
- If you wish, you may begin the affirmation process with the Serenity Prayer:

> God grant me the serenity to accept the things
> I cannot change; the courage to change the things
> I can; and the wisdom to know the difference.

(You may say "grants" to keep the prayer in the present tense.)

Summary

> If you see it as if it were so, and
>   you feel it as if it were so, and
>   you say it as if it were so and
>   you act as if it were so . . .
>   then it is more likely to be so.

8
Getting Ourselves Together

The first priority of a manager is people development, and the means to do so is work.

During the next few weeks, I thought a lot about imagery. The Wizard's story about going "beyond the walls" had new meaning for me. I realized that I was the wall. There were several times when I caught myself thinking of all the reasons why something couldn't be done. I now consciously arrested these thoughts and began to look beyond the problems and think about how it could be done. I found that my mood changed as my thoughts changed. I proved to myself that images give rise to feelings and actions, and what we have in our minds is the determining factor. A new sense of power came over me as I thought about all the possibilities this suggested.

I also noticed that if I imagined the potential of my office staff, my relationship with them changed. I saw them all as having greater value, and they in turn responded to my positive expectation. What the Wizard said was true. When I attended to the image I had in my mind, I brought that potential into being. What extraordinary powers we have that we don't even begin to use! I couldn't wait to share the excitement of these newly-found powers with the Wizard.

When we next met, the Wizard was organizing a treasure

hunt with neighborhood children. "It is a pity adults do not have this much fun at work. Children are natural practitioners of the art of being alive. They develop through play, which is a child's work. Adults develop through work, which should be our form of play. This is what management is all about—getting people *done* through work."

"Getting people *done* through work? What do you mean by that?"

At that moment, several children ran up to the Wizard to ask him to identify what they had found—pinecones, feathers, wild flowers, seeds, leaves, and bark. If they were not objects needed for the treasure hunt, they dropped them immediately and rushed back into the woods to search again. The Wizard seemed to draw energy from the enthusiasm of the children. They were so open, so focused; they were having so much fun. The Wizard said it was because children are fully present and have no mindsets.

The Wizard stepped away from the game to answer my question. "The classic definition of *management* is 'getting work done through people,' but that has the wrong emphasis. Business must strive for both work completion and people development. It is a matter of which comes first. Most managers have work completion as their first priority . . . but because people do the work, they must come first. The first priority of a manager is people development, and the means to do so is through work. That is why I say management is the art of getting people *done* through work."

I gave the Wizard a look of mild amazement. "You always see things a little differently, don't you?"

"That is what creativity is all about—different perceptions. Seeing things differently keeps you out of those insidious mindsets, those self-perpetuating habit loops. Speaking of habits, how have you been doing on imagery and affirmations?" probed the Wizard.

"I really could sense the power of imagination, but I felt rather silly saying those positive things to myself that weren't actually so," I replied, dropping my eyes with embarrassment.

"Anything new seems strange at first. But please realize you do not have any difficulty saying negative affirmations to yourself such as 'I can't do that' or 'That's not my style' or 'I just can't see myself in that situation.' These negative statements are no more real than the positive ones you have trouble saying, yet you have convinced yourself that the negative ones are so. By affirming the negative, you limit yourself to a comfortable mindset, and you feel insecure when circumstance forces you out.

Affirmations are one way to break out, but you have to believe them. Otherwise the process is merely mechanical, and it will not work. It sounds as if you have doubts." The Wizard invited my response.

After a brief pause, I raised my eyes and said, "I guess I do. Any suggestions?"

"Always!" The Wizard was never short on suggestions. "The key to change is awareness, relaxed awareness. Another name for this is concentration."

"I'd like to know more about that. I have trouble concentrating," I admitted.

The Wizard began, "There is a quiet time associated with growth and development. It is a time to get yourself together, to sort yourself out, to open yourself to the energy within and around you, to unify your mind and body. Experience shows that the calmer you are, the more access you have to your creative or intuitive powers. This is not thinking time. It is time to quiet the thinking mind and allow the unconscious mind to work its integrating ways. Imagery and affirmations work best in a quiet, reflective, meditative, prayerful state—a state of relaxed awareness."

"A lot of people like me are wound up most of the time, and we find it hard to wind ourselves down to this state," I complained. "It's hard to convince people like me that this is a useful activity when a situation cries out for decisions and action—like an unhappy client demanding satisfaction or one of my kids testing the limits of my authority."

"The late Joseph Campbell, a mythologist, said, 'An athlete in championship form has a quiet place in himself. It's out of that that his actions come. If he's all in the action field, he's not performing properly.' "

Then with a playful smile, the Wizard said, "An English friend of mine calls this non-stop action 'mindless self-propulsion.' "

I responded with a sense of resignation. "Then I must spend a lot of time mindlessly propelling myself."

"Many business managers never come close to their potential for this very reason. The quiet place in oneself is a preparatory stage for action. Here you heighten and focus your concentration powers. You bring your whole self together into the act. You summon your innermost resources to make your action more powerful and purposeful. The process begins with the physical centering of the body. Have you ever started an activity and found yourself out of rhythm and unable to recover, so you stop and start over?"

I laughed, knowingly. "That happened to me just the other day when I was giving a presentation to my board of directors. I got started wrong and I never did recover. Where were you when I needed you?"

"This happens when you start anything uncentered," acknowledged the Wizard. "Watch a diver before she begins her approach on the board. Notice a gymnast as he mentally prepares himself for his floor routine. They are getting themselves together in stillness so they may summon all their powers for their brief test of athletic and artistic skills."

A smile crept across my face. "You're saying that if I had approached my board with the same centered concentration that the diver approached her board, I wouldn't have had any problems."

The Wizard answered with a smile. "Nice play on words. And you are exactly right. We can learn much from athletes and performing artists. Their success depends largely upon their ability to retain this inner calm of relaxed awareness throughout their performance. The dancer, Jean Erdman, says there is a center out of which you act. That center has to be known and held."

"So this quiet center is not just a preparatory stage—it's a continuing thing as well." I felt I was becoming an accomplished active listener.

"The conscious mind cannot possibly control all the complex moves in these supreme tests of skill. Athletes must rely on their bodies, a wisdom that comes from years of disciplined practice and a relaxed, open awareness to feeling feedback. William Blake said, 'Mechanical excellence is the vehicle for genius.' Genius only comes when you have mastered the mechanics of a discipline. Then when your mind is open to feedback from your body, it will teach itself. Tim Gallwey, author of *Inner Tennis,* says 'If the body knows, let it happen. If it doesn't, let it learn.' " The Wizard paused to give me space.

"And you say this is not a conscious thinking process?" I questioned, cocking my head doubtfully.

"Absolutely not! The time for thinking is before and after you take action, but not during. Gallwey says 'to achieve consistency and accuracy you must become extraordinarily sensitive to feel.' Tennis is too fast and the skills are too complex for the rational thought process. These examples are of athletes acting alone, but think how complex the skills become when you are on a team competing with others. The need for centering is all the greater. The same is true in all forms of human interaction, not just competition."

"I can see that," I exclaimed. "When the diver and the gymnast center themselves physically, they also are centering their minds as well, aren't they?"

"As the British say, you are 'spot on,' " affirmed the Wizard. "You cannot separate the two. The mind and the body are one, so when you alter the mind, you alter the body. You have to take that inner journey first to make the outer journey more focused."

"So the inner journey centers me to make the outer more powerful and purposeful." These brief summaries were my way of checking how well I was understanding.

The Wizard was quick to respond. "Well said! Centering takes you beyond your intellect to your being, beyond what you have learned to be to what you actually are. It takes you to what is. Centeredness is *how to be.*"

It never failed. Whenever I seemed to mentally catch up with the Wizard, he would take me one step beyond. It was a constant game of catch-up. "The inner journey takes me to what *is*? To my being? What then?"

"Your being, that which is authentically you, is open and unbiased. It is pure spirit and has no conscious limitations, no preconceptions. As such, it provides you with the maximum potential for creativity and change." The Wizard's manner was matter-of-fact.

Although this sounded good to me, I really didn't understand it. My question was genuine: "How do I do this?"

The Wizard chose a medical example to give scientific authenticity to this elusive concept of *how to be*. "Dr. Herbert Benson, President of the Mind/Body Institute in Boston, has some insights on this. What began as a process of reducing blood pressure has become a prerequisite for personal renewal. Benson found that the *relaxation response* or *meditation* opened the mind as well as the body to the forces of renewal. He discovered that the relaxation response evokes a greater harmony between the two halves of the brain, it makes it easier to process new information, and it enables us to see situations in new and creative ways. In short, the whole process of relaxation opens us up to change."

Assuming the mind and body are one, I knew the answer to the question I was about to ask, but I wanted to hear the Wizard's version. "Does physical relaxation give me a mental edge as well?"

"No doubt about it. Benson says the response gives anyone greater 'cognitive receptivity.' Another name for this is *beginner's mind,* an open and unbiased outlook. This enables you to approach any situation as a beginner, someone with everything to learn. In a relaxed state, you are most open to new approaches. This is the time to plant new ideas, the time when positive mental imagery and affirmations are more likely to take root and embed themselves in new patterns of behavior."

"It's like a fresh start?"

"For the moment, yes," assured the Wizard. "It is like setting the stopwatch back to zero so you can fully and accurately capture the moment without your prejudices and pre-dispositions getting in the way. A relaxed state of being enables you to consider new initiatives, conflicting points of view, or creative approaches without your conscious mind rejecting them straight away. The unbounded nature of your being makes this possible. The intellect cannot give you a fair hearing. You have to get closer to your true center."

I didn't fully understand yet, but I knew with enough prompting that it would become clearer. "And this is why you call it centering?"

"Precisely. Not an easy thing for people to do, however. You might find it easier to understand if you think about what it means to be uncentered. You are uncentered when you:

- have biases, predispositions, or fixed positions
- feel insecure, guilty, depressed, anxious, or angry
- have unrealistic expectations for your work associates, family, or self
- prescribe "shoulds" for other people
- try to change people exclusively for your own reasons
- allow yourself to be changed exclusively for others' reasons"

I shook my head. "You've just described me. I'm so off-center, it's a wonder I'm still upright!" With that, I suddenly jumped up on the trunk of a fallen Norway pine and extended my arms for balance. Carefully placing one foot in front of the other, I teetered uneasily for a few feet before losing my balance and jumping off. Turning to the Wizard and grinning with childlike glee, I asked, "Does this mean I'm psychologically unbalanced as well?"

The Wizard laughed heartily. He was obviously delighted. It was a sign I was less tense and feeling more comfortable with myself. "I feel better already!" I exclaimed.

"There is nothing like physical exertion," the Wizard said. "We are all uncentered to some degree. The problem with being uncentered, however, is that you see the world through your own depressed, anxious, or frustrated eyes. As such, you mix your own personal needs with the demands of the situation. You create, in effect, a self-inflicted crises and you suffer needless tension with non-problems, problems that would not be present if you took the time to center yourself."

"Needless tension with non-problems—that's the story of our times, isn't it, Wizard? If I could only bring my balanced self to each situation I face, I would eliminate most of my problems."

"This is why using your imagination is so important," stressed the Wizard, who was now drawing on our last encounter. "If you can envision what you would like to achieve, nearly every obstacle is a non-problem. In the context of a vision, any problem is simply a non-event. Having a vision channels your energy and enables you to transcend problems that would block others."

I then made a powerful observation. "What I really face is not the problems but my attitude toward those problems—and that is a choice that is up to me to make."

"Yes, and that is a choice no one can take from you—the right to choose your own attitude. Victor Frankl, author of *Man's Search for Meaning* and a holocaust survivor, calls this choice the last of the human freedoms. Nobody can put you down unless you allow it. If you feel put down, that is your choice. Other choices of how to feel, however, are available to you. This is what Selye meant when he said it is not what happens to you that hurts you, but how you take it."

"It takes a very centered person to make those choices," I acknowledged with some futility in my voice.

"When you are uncentered, another person's untoward behavior can be a big problem for you," reasoned the Wizard. "To a centered person, however, the same problem may be dismissed as a mere eccentricity.

"The word eccentric means off-center. The behavior is 'off-center,' but it does not create a problem for the centered person. Eccentricity is part of the tapestry of life and at worst, it is an irritation. When you are balanced it takes a pretty solid hit to knock you off-balance. Whereas if you start off-balance, it does not take much to throw you even more off-center. Furthermore, when you start in-balance, you have a greater capacity to right yourself. The centered person is like a self-righting rescue ship. These ships are virtually incapable of capsizing."

I responded excitedly, "In England I've watched the ships from the Royal National Lifeboat Institute practice rescues. They're incredibly resilient. When they roll over, they roll right back!"

"The resilience of a centered person stems from the act of centering, and that is an energizing process. It is a restorative process that prepares you both to give and to receive energy. The power of centering lies in your ability to summon and to channel your energies for any occasion. I cannot make this point too strongly for business managers." The Wizard's tone became more serious.

"I am not advocating the monastic, introspective life for you, although that option is open to anyone. If you do not understand this process and if you fail to use it effectively, you risk being victimized by external events and circumstances. You become fodder, consumed by problems and crises. This is the trap many of us are in. I mentioned that earlier when we talked about urgent versus important matters."

"I'm glad you tied it back to that. It's all connected, isn't it? I really have to ask myself, Am I managing my business, or is my business managing me?"

"Yes, and without parents centering themselves, their families could turn from safe havens of support to scenes of abusive behavior, addiction, and despair. Just as athletes prepare by centering themselves, you should also center yourself for a meeting, a family outing, a confrontation, a negotiation, or whatever. Centering readies you to receive energy by opening yourself to your own creative source and to the energy of others. It also readies you to give by enhancing the quality of energy that emanates from you. This mutual exchange of energies is what managing business, family, and self is all about. To me, it is the placebo effect working its magic in management, just as it has always worked in medicine. This is the real secret of management, the untold story that will have to wait for another time. Waiting. . . ." the Wizard chuckled. "That is the way life is."

Suggestions

Add these relaxation and centering ideas that the Wizard gave to me to your positive affirmations and mental imagery practice:

- As you move from one situation to another, take time to pause between them, even if just for a moment. This may be done at your desk between meetings or even in a meeting. Sit comfortably, nothing crossed, with hands in your lap or resting on your thighs. Take several deep breaths, breathing through your nose. Briefly, hold the breaths, then exhale slowly. Clear your mind of all the events that preceded this breathing. Be conscious of any muscle tension. Relax any tense muscles. You will begin to feel your body metabolism slowing down.

With practice, you can relax in just a few moments. At the appropriate time, you may begin to think about the next business encounter. Before you begin, visualize the outcome as you would like it to be. See it working out as you want it to. When you are ready, begin to take action to achieve the desired outcome.

In *Your Maximum Mind,* Dr. Herbert Benson recommends the following "Relaxation Response" as crucial in practically any self-help program:

Step 1—Pick a focus word or short phrase firmly rooted in your personal belief system. For example, words like "love" or "one."

Step 2—Sit quietly in a comfortable position.

Step 3—Close your eyes.

Step 4—Relax your muscles.

Step 5—Breathe slowly and naturally, and repeat your focus word to yourself as you exhale.

Step 6—Assume a passive attitude. When a distracting thought enters your mind, gently bring your attention back to a focus word. Don't judge, and don't worry about how well you're doing.

Step 7—Continue for 10–20 minutes. Practice this entire Seven-Step process once or twice daily.

9
The Doctor Within

When you fulfill the belief that others have in you,
you discover the strength that lies within.

What a difference words make! I kept reflecting on the Wizard's definition of management: getting people *done* through work. It's true that developing people is what management is all about. This new perception began to change the way I managed people. I could see clearly that changing my perception changed the way I did things. The mental images I had of my staff were changing, and so were my feelings and actions toward them.

I remembered what the Wizard had said earlier about healing and helping people become more whole. Getting people *done* through work is healing and making people whole. I realized, however, that I had much work to do on myself. My daily routine was so frenetic that I found I didn't always take the time to center myself between activities. But when I did, I noticed that things seemed to go a little smoother. Perhaps it was coincidental, but I felt a little more in control of things when I took a few moments to get myself together. Routinely centering myself was something I would have to work on, but I could definitely see merit in it.

In those quiet meditative moments, I did take some time to practice positive mental imagery in areas where I had been previously negative. I focused on my health worries first, and slowly turned away from fear and despair. A new sense of optimism and a feeling of euphoria began to emerge along with my positive affirmations of life. I had always been told how difficult it was for people to change themselves, but I was finding this whole process to be a quietly transforming experience. I liked what was happening to me and I liked what was happening to the people I worked with.

When we next met, the Wizard had just finished his usual lunch of fruits, whole grain foods, and fresh garden vegetables.

"How are your eating habits coming?" He asked me.

"Much better. I feel healthier and less distressed these days. And I feel that I have more energy."

"Nutrition does play a vital role in that regard."

"Speaking of energy, the last time we met you talked about the energy we exchange with others," I reminded, "and then you mentioned an 'untold story.'"

"You remembered!"

"How could I forget, Wizard, especially if it's as important as you say?"

"Sometimes I get a bit carried away with my statements, but there are some rather simple and profound truths about people, and I believe this is one of them. It is, perhaps, the real magic of management."

"I'm ready when you are."

The Wizard said, "When medical people refer to a *placebo,* do you know what they mean?"

"I believe so. That's the sugar pill, isn't it?"

"Yes, but it is much more than that."

"With you, it always is," I needled.

The two of us shared a laugh as the Wizard offered me a slice of his honeydew melon.

"This is the real reason why I keep coming to see you," I joked, savoring the sweetness of the melon. "But what else is a placebo?"

"It is any pill, potion, or procedure that has no direct effect on a patient's illness," said the Wizard, "but the patient believes it will work."

"So it's not the pill itself but the patient that makes the real difference?"

"Precisely." The Wizard seemed pleased. "The great British physician, Sir William Osler, said it was more important to know what *person* has a disease than what *disease* a person has. The idea is to treat people, not diseases."

"So it's a matter of where the doctor puts his energies, on the disease or on the patient?"

"Yes. The same mistake is made in education when we teach courses rather than people, or sell products rather than customers." The Wizard loved to make comparisons.

"You've identified a very subtle difference," I allowed.

"My use of language is subtle, but the difference is quite immense. Many scholars believe the history of medicine is the history of the placebo effect. What is important is not just the treatment, but the patient's belief that the treatment will work. If they see themselves recovering, then these innocuous little potions work their wondrous ways as often as 70% of the time."

"So what does all this placebo talk have to do with management?" I challenged.

"Plenty," insisted the Wizard. "You see, the belief can be as important as the treatment. A placebo is really an image of healing in the mind of the patient. The image transforms itself into healing through that three-step process you and I discussed some time ago."

"You mean the image-feeling-action cycle?"

"Precisely."

"We talked then about using mental imagery to break old habit patterns, to see new possibilities, and to go 'beyond the walls.' Now you're saying a placebo is imagery, and it also has healing powers?"

The Wizard explained, "Mental imagery is one way you 'talk' to your body. The other way is through your emotions. Positive emotions and positive imagery stimulate the healing process. The science of PNI, psychoneuroimmunology, is breaking new ground in linking emotions to the immune system. In this context, imagination, or mental imagery, is the greatest healer. It is the magical nexus that holds the body and the mind together."

"What I have on my mind affects how I feel and what I do," I remembered.

"If you can psyche yourself into getting sick, you can also psyche yourself into getting well and staying well," continued the Wizard. "We know that negative emotions such as depression and anxiety weaken the immune system, while positive emotions such as love and forgiveness strengthen it. If you see yourself getting better with positive expectations, then you are setting the stage for the body to heal itself. An estimated 85% of all people seeking medical help suffer from self-limiting disorders well within their capabilities to heal themselves."

"85%?" I reacted with surprise.

"Yes, the late Franz Inglefinger, editor of the *New England Journal of Medicine,* wrote that 85% of human illnesses are within reach of the body's own healing system. Remember, doctors do not heal. They are only channels. In effect, a doctor simply gives you permission to heal yourself. Putting it more accurately, you give yourself permission. All healing is self-healing in this regard. The best medical help is only as good as the images our mind will allow."

"Once again, it's up to us," I said. "So my negative images can negate positive medical intervention. . . ."

"The late Norman Cousins concluded ten years of mind-body research by saying, 'Patients tend to move along the path of their expectations, whether on the upside or on the downside,' " recounted the Wizard. "Often, the patient's mindset disallows medical help."

"Are you saying that the placebo is a patient's positive expectation?"

"Yes, all of the helping professions are alike in that they encourage patients to take charge of their lives and do something positive for themselves," said the Wizard. "When asked what a doctor could do, one well-known surgeon suggested two things: first, the doctor could give patients control over their own treatment; and second, the doctor could offer hope."

I'm sure I looked a little stunned. "That's amazing, coming from a surgeon. It sounds more like good management advice—turn the job over to your staff and demonstrate your confidence in them to do it."

"You just made the management connection you asked about earlier, and you are right. That *is* good advice. If you are programmed with habitually self-defeating images of yourself, the treatment simply will not work. When you replace negative images with positive ones, you redirect your energies toward healing. The job of the doctor is to open the patient to the process of healing," avowed the Wizard.

"The placebo is obviously a lot more than I thought it was," I confessed.

"The placebo comes in three stages," the Wizard explained. "The first and most elementary stage is the pill itself. Most people need something tangible like taking a pill or getting a shot to equate with getting well. It tells you that some physical good will come of this. A prescription from a doctor you trust is tangible assurance of getting well."

"It makes sense that if my symptoms are tangible, I ought to deal with them tangibly—with a pill," I agreed.

"That is the easiest connection for most people to make. The second placebo stage involves only the relationship with the doctor. At this stage, all you need is reassurance. The effect hinges on the confidence you have in the doctor and in your conviction that the doctor takes you seriously. Here, the doctor is the placebo. More specifically, the placebo is the quality of the relationship between you and the doctor. Your belief that the doctor cares makes you receptive to suggestion. Francis Peabody said, 'The secret of the care of the patient is in caring for the patient.'"

"Here all we need is the doctor's word?"

"Or the doctor's touch. When a mother kisses her child's skinned knee, she is performing a healing act. She is the placebo."

I smiled knowingly. "Well, I'm beginning to see the connection."

"There is more," said the Wizard. "The third and highest

placebo stage takes place within you," declared the Wizard. "At this level you do not need tangible effects or even reassurance. Instead of needing externals, your intuitive sense tells you what is best. Norman Cousins, in his classic book *Anatomy of an Illness,* recalls Dr. Albert Schweitzer telling him one of medicine's secrets: 'Each patient carries his own doctor inside him. They come to us not knowing the truth. We are at our best when we give the doctor who resides within each patient a chance to go to work.' At this stage, the placebo is the 'doctor within.' "

"That is the first thing you told me when we met," I recollected. "The answers you seek lie within you."

"I am gratified that you remember," said the Wizard. "All three placebo stages have one thing in common—a *belief* in recovery. All have the expectation, the hope, and the will to recover. Belief is much more powerful than any external technique."

"Belief is more powerful than technique," I repeated. "That statement is powerful."

"It is powerful because you believe it. I believe the placebo effect works in all the healing professions. The doctor, the therapist, the coach, the teacher, the business manager, the parent—all have placebo power. The vast majority of people are at the first placebo stage. At this stage, they need *things* to help them feel okay about themselves. They need to validate their worth externally because they are not sure of themselves internally. Status symbols are the big consideration here. These are the 'sugar pills' of management. You recall in *The Wizard of Oz,* the Cowardly Lion received a medal for bravery from Oz. He wanted courage, and this was tangible evidence. The medal was the placebo.

"Significantly fewer people operate at the second placebo stage. Here they only need the *reassurance* of the manager, the healing touch. This reinforcing or reaffirming act is a vital and continuous part of the management process. At stage two, the manager is the placebo.

"Very few people have reached the point where they are able to function fully and effectively at the third placebo stage. This level requires faith, a strong sense of personal worth, and a confidence that comes from the inner journey. At this stage, they do not need external reassurance in the form of things and people. They know intuitively what to do."

"Why the need for stage three? Why not just give people management 'pills' at stage one and be done with it?" I quizzed the Wizard. "Surely you aren't saying we should forsake the tangibles like pay and perks and toys for some hoped-for internal satisfaction."

"Far from it," argued the Wizard. "Everyone wants to embrace life fully. You and your staff need the tangibles and the reassurances from the people you admire and respect. The idea, if you recall, is to turn the treatment over to the patient. If you do not move beyond the first two placebo stages, you will forever be dependent upon others. It is only by reaching stage three that you can live freely at the other two. Then you do not have to have them. If you do not have to have something, you are then free to choose what is best for you. You are less likely to be victimized by those who exploit and manipulate these rewards for their own purposes. You are not dependent on things or on others. The 'doctor within' prescribes what is best for you."

"Now I see what you mean. The pill is only a short-term fix. Presumably, the only way I can erase my dependency is to develop my inner resources—what you call the 'doctor within.'"

"Precisely! You want to get beyond the debilitating constraints of dependency," urged the Wizard. "Our age of specialization is an age of fragmentation. You have learned helplessness, an acquired dependence on specialists. Medicine is just one of those specialties. You need to re-establish control over your own life. This is what the 'doctor within' can do for you. You need doctors and other specialists, but the locus of control in your life must remain with you. You cannot abdicate that responsibility. Passively taking placebo pills does not prepare you to accept that responsibility."

"That's a lesson we need to learn in business," I injected.

"You are so right. Developing your inner resources gives you the strength to avoid becoming a victim of power games. If you need something—like keeping your job or getting respect—that others control, they have power over you and they could take advantage of you."

"That's very unsettling. . . ."

"Yes," said the Wizard, "and sadly, control is the basis of much organizational insecurity in the business world, not to mention power struggles between parents and children. Management by fear has always been with us. It is premised on making you feel you have no choice but to comply. However, if you value what others do for you but you do not have to do it, then you have options. This enables you to work with others more creatively by not being a victim of their power games."

The Wizard excused himself from the room for a moment. When he returned, he offered me a glass of his hand-pressed apple cider. I raised the glass to toast my host and eyed its turbid contents. "Mm-m-m-m! That has so much more flavor than the clear cider." Reflecting on the Wizard's comment about not being a victim, I mused, "We always come back to our inner selves, don't we?"

"The answers you seek . . ." the Wizard began.

". . . lie within you," I finished. "It makes more sense to me now than the first time I heard it. But I have a question for you: If very few of us function at this inner stage three, what are my chances for developing the 'doctor within'?"

"There is always hope," said the Wizard with a look of expectancy. "Hope itself is a powerful placebo. Alone, it has healing powers that make you receptive to change."

"But what can I specifically do as a manager?"

"Exercise placebo power at all three stages," declared the Wizard. "Cover the needs at stage one with the necessary tangibles, the material things. Be a living placebo at stage two with your 'touch.' And get people *done* through work at stage three. Offer your workforce the opportunity to develop themselves by making a difference in your company. This involves all that we have talked about and more—energizing possibilities, balancing the urgent and the important, learning the power of concentration to unify inner calm and outer action, releasing your energy, and opening yourself to the energies of others. It is a lifetime job. But what an exciting one it is! Everything your people do on the job is an investment in themselves. They are literally 'self-employed' within the company, and that is the best of both worlds."

"Wizard, I think I've got it, but could you sum this up just one more time? It is all so new to me!"

"At stage one, you need *things* to tell you that you are okay. This is blatantly apparent in America, where people need monogrammed clothing to convince themselves and others that they belong. At stage two, you need *people* whom you respect to reassure you that you are okay. At stage three, you have weaned yourself away from being dependent upon externals. Here, *you know intuitively* that you have worth and are okay. The 'doctor within' has told you so. Your job then, as a manager, is to use your placebo power to help others free themselves by getting beyond the dependency of the first two stages. Placebo power gives you a three-stage process for developing the 'doctor within.' It is the real magic of management, indeed, of life itself," concluded the Wizard.

"I know I have a long way to go, yet if you hadn't believed in me, I would never have come this far. You've helped me at a very stressful time in my life. I owe you a lot, Wizard."

"You owe me nothing, but you owe your staff something. Do for them as you say I have done for you," urged the Wizard. "It all begins with belief in a person's potential. When you believe in the potential of others, you energize that potential. You *potentiate* people, empowering them to release their energies and go 'beyond the walls.' This is placebo power, the enduring message in *The Wizard of Oz.* When you fulfill the belief that others have in you, you will surely discover the strength that lies within. That strength is the 'doctor within,' and that is *how to be.*"

"Thank you. I appreciate hearing how I can grow and help others, too."

"You are most welcome. Building your practice for the

'doctor within' demands that you employ powers of the mind vastly superior to your rational powers. I refer to the 'irrational' power of intuition. But now my 'doctor within' tells me that is a story for another time. That is the way life is."

Suggestions

The Wizard had me ask myself and others the following questions:

- Stage One—What are some tangible placebos I need to confirm my okay-ness?
- Stage Two—Who are some of the people I depend upon to reassure me of my okay-ness?
- Stage Three—What do I need from myself and from others to develop my "doctor within"?

Ask the following questions concerning your key people at work:

- Stage One—What tangible placebos can I administer to them to confirm their okay-ness?
- Stage Two—What intangible placebos can I personally offer to reassure them of their okay-ness?
- Stage Three—What are some things I can do to help them develop their "doctor within"?

Give each person the first three questions you asked yourself.

Have them reflect upon them for a day or so while you ask yourself the second set of three questions.

Compare your "findings" with theirs.

Use the questions and responses as the basis for a personal development discussion with each person individually.

10
The Curse of Consciousness

*The curse of consciousness is to see the world
in bits and pieces.*

I was quite moved by my latest visit with the Wizard. First, I decided to take more time to reflect on the power of belief and my "doctor within." I felt a greater sense of aliveness as I accepted the challenge of moving my staff from their near total dependency on me and on material, tangible things to the inner confidence that I was beginning to experience. I knew if I was to be the healer in all of my interactions with them, in my "manager" role, I must be a whole person. If doctors practice medicine, I must practice management. It was, of course, crucial to my own health and well-being that I heal myself in the process.

Practicing implies developing one's skills. Even the most accomplished physicians, musicians, and athletes continue to practice. Practice makes them more complete, more whole. There were moments when I actually felt like *I* was the Wizard because of the connections I was making. These were heady times. My mind was swimming as I thought about all the how-to-be ideas from my meetings with the Wizard. I was excited about the possibilities opening in my life. What the Wizard said about possibilities was really true: They do excite!

I could feel a difference in myself now, compared to the frustration and fatigue I felt a few months ago when I sought out the Wizard. Recalling the Wizard's statement that the answers lay within me, I now realized they were beginning to emerge as the "doctor within."

One dark cloud loomed on my horizon. For some time I had a sore on the back of my left hand that resisted healing. As a young person I spent a lot of time in the sun and, being fair-skinned, I had the potential for developing skin cancer in later years. The Wizard had made me more aware of my overall health. It was time I did something about this.

Several weeks passed before we met again. When we did, it was as if no time had gone by. The Wizard said that was the mark of a good relationship. A light rain was falling as the two of us moved into his house. The Wizard built a fire in the study while I told him how much better I was feeling and the deep stirring of excitement and hope I felt inside.

"It sounds as if the 'doctor within' is making rounds," the Wizard noted, his face alive with satisfaction. "I am so pleased you are having this renaissance of feelings, for this is what will stir you to take positive action. And action is what a manager's life is all about."

"Last time, you said that in order to build my practice for the 'doctor within,' I needed to employ intuition—an 'irrational' power greater than reason." I fixed my eyes on the Wizard wondering what he really meant. "That struck me as a rather curious statement."

"It is curious, isn't it?" admitted the Wizard. "Let me tell you a story about the first enemy engagement of the Falklands War, the battle of Goose Green. It was daybreak 28 May, 1982, and enemy fire threatened to overwhelm 2 Para, the elite British second Battalion Parachute Regiment. In an attempt to break the impasse and sensing his position would deteriorate further with daylight, battalion commander Colonel H. Jones charged the well entrenched Argentine position in a gallant, solitary assault up Darwin Hill. He was killed instantly.

Second in command Major Chris Keeble, receiving the

army's coded signal, 'Sunray's down,' assumed leadership in broad daylight on bare terrain. Outgunned and outmanned nearly four to one the British situation deteriorated as the day wore on. At dusk it seemed retreat was the only option. The men in his battalion pressed Major Keeble for a decision. Unwilling to retreat and not knowing what else to do, he walked a few steps away from his men. In a small ravine, alone with his thoughts, he said a short prayer: 'My Father, I abandon myself to you. Do with me as you will. I am ready for anything. I accept everything provided your will is fulfilled in me. I ask for nothing more.'

"As Major Keeble tells the story, he was immediately suffused with a feeling of peacefulness and hope and, for the first time since the battalion had landed, he was not aware of the biting cold. In those few quiet moments, the germ of an amazing idea came to him. Why not a peaceful solution? Here were two Christian forces killing each other. It was madness. His idea, incongruous as it seemed to be, was to offer the enemy commander a surrender with honor! His message would be love, not bloodshed.

"When he returned to his men and presented his idea, they thought he was mad, but he persisted. Working with his signalman, Major Keeble released two prisoners with a message requesting to meet the enemy commander. When they met, the enemy officers appeared in spotless dress uniforms, while he and his officers 'reeked of violence and death' in full combat gear. Major Keeble, with steely-eyed will, told the commander that his second Battalion had come 10,000 miles and were not about to stop 100 yards short of their goal. The enemy was given the option of a surrender with honors in a full dress parade, or be overwhelmed. The Argentine commander accepted the offer, and the British regiment celebrated its first victory of the war."

"Astonishing! But why would the Argentineans surrender when they were winning?" I wondered.

"Perhaps they did not know they were winning; but that is not the point," said the Wizard. "Let us not lose sight of the purpose of the story. Without open space, that quiet meditative moment, the germ of a peaceful solution would not have flowered. Major Keeble could not even have perceived it. The solution was not the result of rational thought. It was intuitive or 'irrational.' We cannot summon intuition as we can summon reason. To employ the power of intuition, we can only prepare ourselves to receive it."

"You've certainly piqued my interest."

"I fear I must get a bit theoretical again. Can a person of action like you stand another metaphysical discourse?" the Wizard asked, in a mock-professorial manner.

"I've survived your other talks without serious side effects," I replied, with arms outstretched and eyes cast downward, pretending to scan my body for negative side effects. "Try me once more."

The Wizard rose from his chair to attend to the fire. He placed three logs pyramid-style on top of the kindling which, by now, was burning well. Then he settled back into his chair, winked at me to soften the seriousness, and began to speak.

"Nature has no walls. The natural world you live in is an unbroken whole, a seamless panorama. But because the whole is too vast for the conscious mind to grasp, you are blessed with five senses and an analytical mind to fathom this whole. With these faculties, you can literally break the natural world into bite-size pieces to make sense of it.

"You see it, touch it, hear it, taste it, smell it, and analyze it in detail to know more about it. We call this process *differentiation*, breaking down the whole into different parts. Your conscious mind looks for differences. It discriminates one thing from another by separation—different shapes, colors, sounds, and so on. But this blessing is also a curse. The *curse of consciousness* is to see the world in its separateness, to constantly perceive it in bits and pieces."

"Curse of consciousness?"

"Consciousness separates," said the Wizard. "Therefore, to integrate the pieces of the world into a whole, you must get beyond the conscious mind, beyond the limitation of your senses. That is what intuition does for you.

"Over the millennia, humans have developed a certain wisdom in surviving. For example, the body copes with stress and immunizes itself against foreign substances. This wisdom of the body is programmed into your genetic inheritance. Because we cannot separate mind from body, your mind has this wisdom in the unconscious state. Jung called this universal mind the collective unconscious. This wisdom, too, is part of your endowment. In this context, you 'know' all you need to know from the beginning. This is the wisdom of the ages. The key question is, how can you access it?

"Intuition alone has access to the unconscious mind, that limitless unknown that lies beyond your consciousness. It has the power of integration, the capacity to synthesize the fragments of the conscious mind with glimpses of insight into the whole of life. Where the rational, conscious mind separates the whole, the 'irrational,' unconscious mind integrates it. This is the mind's true healing power."

"How can I access all that intuitive healing power?" I asked. "It would . . . come in handy."

"Everything begins with awareness, yet to be aware of anything, you must first bring it to your consciousness. Do you know who controls your conscious mind?" The Wizard liked to answer questions with questions.

"My boss!" I said laughingly. Then in a quick reversal of mood, I became serious again. "No. Who?"

"You said that lightly, I know," observed the Wizard, "but the power to choose your own state of mind is the last of the human freedoms. It is frightening how readily many of us relinquish this right on a regular basis."

"I know all too well," I said, sounding a bit victimized. "That's why I have to develop my 'doctor within.' It sounds as if intuition and the 'doctor within' have a lot in common. But, I apologize—you were about to tell me who controls my conscious mind. . . ."

"I am glad you distracted me for a bit—I love distractions. They are often more productive than the subject that gives rise to them. But here is the answer to your question: The CEO of your conscious mind is the *ego*. For you to be aware of anything, it must first pass through your consciousness, and that is under the tight supervision of the ego. Intuition does not stand a chance—it simply does not function—as long as the ego is in charge."

"Now that's power!" I said with a knowing smile.

"You bet it is, and do not think for a moment that the ego hesitates to use the power," said the Wizard, pointing his finger in a commanding manner. "I believe this is management's biggest problem. This is also a parent's greatest downfall."

"Ego is the biggest problem?"

"Yes," declared the Wizard, "Ego has created numberless problems throughout history. Joseph Campbell taught us that dragons and other ogres are common to all cultures. The hero must slay the dragon, symbolic of the ego, to continue the personal journey. The mythic passage symbolizes what we call the inner journey.

"Campbell wrote, 'It has always been the prime function of mythology and rite to supply the symbols that carry the human spirit forward.' Myths teach us symbolically how to take the human spirit forward with the inner journey. Scientific materialism has de-mythologized our culture and obliterated the historic benchmarks for the inner journey. Furthermore, scientific thinking has reduced us to our smallest component parts. As a result of this reductionism, the growth of the human spirit has been stunted.

"In business and in the home, our excessive need for control stunts the spirit. The spirit needs release, not control. Overly authoritative parents stifle the development of a child's creative powers. This process of suppression continues when controlling managers pick up where parents left off. This is the work of the ego, which has a need to control its turf. Because it cannot control the unconscious, which is the source of intuition, it ignores it or demeans it. In doing so, the ego denies itself access to its vast integrative powers.

"The ego has another more immediate problem. Unable to see beyond the fragments of life, the ego assumes that the pieces are the whole. When another person's ego sees different bits, the two argue endlessly over bits and pieces. Do you recall that wonderful childhood fable about the blind men and the elephant?"

The Wizard reached up and pulled a colorful volume of children's fables from his bookshelf. Smiling, he turned to me and said, "This should be a part of everyone's library. Six blind men, each with a grasp on a different part of the elephant, made a comparison—tusk like a spear, tail like a rope, trunk like a snake, ear like a fan, side like a wall, and knee like a tree."

With that, he riffled through the pages, adjusted his glasses, and read the conclusion to *The Blind Men and the Elephant* by John Geoffrey Saxe:

> And so these men of Indostan
> Disputed loud and long,
> Each in his own opinion
> Exceeding stiff and strong,
> Though each was partly in the right
> And all were in the wrong.
>
> As oft in theologic wars
> The disputants, I ween,
> Rail on in utter ignorance
> Of what each other mean,
> And prate about an elephant
> Not one of them has seen.

"Such wisdom, and written over 100 years ago!" exclaimed the Wizard. "All of us are guilty of 'prating' about the elephant of life that no one has 'seen.' We are experts on the tusk and the tail, but we know almost nothing of the whole. We know how to make a living, but not how to make a life. We know almost nothing of *how to be* in life."

"How do we see the whole?" I asked.

The Wizard drew an imaginary sword from his side, saying, "Suppress the ego." Then he thrust the sword home with a playful shout of, "Slay the dragon!" Sheathing his make-believe weapon, he continued. "You have to open yourself to the reality that your perception is but a small part, only a piece of the whole, and acknowledge that others can contribute more pieces with their perceptions. Rather than fighting over who is right, you can accept that each of us is only partly in the right, but together we can grasp more of the whole. That makes the business manager more respectful of other co-workers."

Once again I probed. "And how do we do this?"

"I think that there are two preconditions," answered the Wizard. "One is to accept full responsibility for yourself. This requires confidence in your own intuition, the placebo power of the 'doctor within.' A great spokesman for this confident spirit is Vaclav Havel, the dissident playwright who became the first president of the new Czech Republic."

Searching through a well-thumbed reading pile, the Wizard pulled out a yellowing newspaper. Moving his finger quickly down the columns, he briefly stopped and smiled, obviously enjoying a passage. At last he found the part he was looking for.

"Speaking to a joint session of the U. S. Congress, Havel said, 'We are still incapable of understanding that the only genuine backbone of all our actions, if they are to be moral, is responsibility—responsibility to something higher than my family, my country, my company, my success. If I subordinate my political behavior to this imperative, mediated to me by my conscience, I can't go far wrong.'

"Your conscience, what you know to be true, will keep your ego in check. Havel has enormous integrity because, at great personal sacrifice, he never accepted communist rule."

"He backed his words with deeds," I agreed. "You said there were *two* preconditions. . . ."

"Yes, of course. Thank you. The other precondition is open space. Everyone needs time to reflect upon the moral responsibility Havel talks about. When you urge people to accept the baton of responsibility, they need time and space to integrate what it really means. This is creative, unstructured time. The concept has to travel from the head to the heart, for the heart is the only place where we truly *know*. Blaise Pascal, the seventeenth-century French mathematician and philosopher said, 'The heart has its own reasons which Reason does not know.'

"The heart will tell us *how to be.* So long as the concept of self-responsibility is only an idea in our heads, it is fragile and easily replaced by a better idea. The heart is our spirit, the center of the self, the goal of our inner journey, the core of our being. When the heart knows, commitment follows."

"That's heavy."

"It is also very relevant," claimed the Wizard. "You are talking about knowing what's right and doing it. Your conscience knows right from wrong. To Havel, it is a choice 'to live within the truth.' In his essay, 'The Power of the Powerless,' he writes about the 'singular, explosive, incalculable power' of this hidden sphere of truth which grows from within, with a life lived openly in the truth."

I barely held on to a thin thread of understanding, but I continued to ask my trademark practical questions. "And how do I know 'the truth'?"

"You have to sort it out for yourself," said the Wizard. "That is Havel's message, and that is what taking responsibility is all about. To be responsible requires space for personal reflection."

The Wizard put another log on the fire and then momentarily excused himself. He returned with a handful of seed corn. Laying it on the table in front of me, he said, "I will plant these different strains of seed corn in the spring. In a memorable speech that led to the first nuclear test ban, President Kennedy said, 'If we cannot end now our differences, at least we can help make the world safe for diversity.'

"With differences comes diversity, and diversity is as vital to the health of society as it is to agriculture. In nature, diversity insures survival. The different genetic strains of this corn will guarantee its survival. So it is with ideas. In the 1980s and early 1990s, the total collapse of communism all across Eastern Europe was due to the absence of political diversity. The challenge today is to manage diversity by allowing the free expression of differences. In effect, this means de-managing or exercising less control. This is a threat to ego, the great turf protector. Managers—everyone—need to learn to let go."

"Let go of what?"

"Ego. Control. Fear. Inhibitions. Stress. Habits. Old ways of doing things. This need to let go is a curious paradox. In letting go, you actually gain control of a different kind. You acquire the energies and commitments of those whom you allow to participate. The key is in allowing, not in controlling, however. Orchestrating this participative diversity is one of the biggest challenges for leadership today, and knowing when to let go is critical. The latter requires humility."

"Humility?"

"Yes," said the Wizard. "Managers who have all the answers do not need others except to carry out their wishes . . . but that day is gone. Metaphorically speaking, you cannot add water to a full glass. Humility is emptying your 'glass' for the moment, so that you may be open to anything."

"So humility is openness?"

"That is a good part of it," said the Wizard. "We all think we are open, but few of us really are. Humility is the 'beginner's mind.' If you know it all, you cannot learn anything new. That is the problem the ego has. Experts are also vulnerable. It is impossible to become a true expert if you already think you are. Certainty gets in the way by closing down awareness. If you are absolutely certain, you are no longer open. Ashley Montagu says, 'Only absolute fools are absolutely certain.'

"Remember, the images you have inside you overpower the images that come from the outside. So you have to neutralize those internal mindsets to get an unbiased perception. That is why we need a heavy dose of humility. This may sound a bit old-fashioned, but humility is truly a timeless quality. Being humble is *how to be*. That is the way life is."

Suggestions

Creativity cannot be summoned on command. The Wizard said I had to be more allowing. Here is his approach:

- If you have an important decision to make or a big problem to solve, immerse yourself in the situation. Concentrate totally and soak up all the information you can.
- After a period of intense effort, if the answers are not forthcoming, don't force them. Through intense concentration, you have told your unconscious mind that this is important.
- Now take time to "sleep on it." If sleep is not appropriate, walk away from it and let your unconscious mind work its wondrous ways while you pursue something trivial or leisurely. This is the critical incubation stage of creativity.
- Answers manifest themselves often in strange ways, so be open to all signs and signals. Insight usually comes in flashes. It cannot be coerced, nor controlled. It can only be allowed to happen. This is often in a relaxed moment when we least expect it.
- If nothing happens, take another run at the decision or problem when you are fresh, and then repeat the process. Insights will come. Your task is simply to be sufficiently relaxed and aware to notice these answers from within.

11

The Dragon Slayer

Einstein had humility because he had a "beginner's mind."

It was a difficult time for me in the weeks that followed. My fears about skin cancer were confirmed. The doctor called and said the biopsies showed malignancy. Immediately I had the lesion surgically removed. This form of skin carcinoma is life-threatening only if it has spread. The doctors were very optimistic, but there was no way yet of knowing if it had. It was impossible tuning out these health concerns and my business worries—intuition was eluding me. I understood what the Wizard said about responsibility, but open space was very elusive. Presumably, intuition comes when I give myself some space, like the account of Major Keeble in the Falklands. Was this the same as the "doctor within"?

It took many days for me to finally settle down. Then I prayed for my own healing and the healing of those around me. Perhaps that did some good, for I began to feel calmer. I still had lots of questions, but for the first time I was mentally able to reconstruct our last session so I could anticipate the next level of healing the Wizard would introduce.

I began talking to myself: "Apparently my conscious mind can't deal with the vast whole of nature. With its analytical reasoning powers, my mind breaks the natural world down into separate components. As a result, I learn more and more about less and less. To make sense out of this, I need to integrate these bits back into the larger context of life. The Hindu fable illustrated that the tusk of an elephant has meaning only in the context of the whole animal. Intuition can provide me with access to the "elephant of life" by giving me fleeting glimpses of the whole. This is the *gestalt,* the illumination stage in the creative process. It is that moment when everything comes together in one flash of insight."

I continued talking to myself: "Nothing comes to my consciousness except through the ego. For my intuition to work, I have to neutralize the ego. Apparently that's the role of humility."

I was relieved that I could recall the essence of what I thought the Wizard had said. More important, for the first time I was able to anticipate what I thought the Wizard was going to say next. When I heard him mention the word humility, I didn't have a beginner's mind. I had always passed the word off lightly like Churchill did when he spoke derisively of a Labor prime minister having "much to be humble about."

I realized that I had been biased against humility. My conscious mind had not given humility a fair hearing. And I definitely was not centered. Consciously, I now allowed my beginner's mind to explore other interpretations of humility and its *how-to-be* importance. In the past I would have taken my bias to the Wizard, laid it out for him, then waited to be convinced otherwise—which only the Wizard could do. It was reassuring to know how I had caught myself this time, without being reminded. And then it struck me—the "doctor within" was at work! A quiet sense of satisfaction came over me. I closed my eyes and savored the moment.

When we next met, the Wizard had some photos spread on the table before him. He invited me to join him at the table. "Have you been on a trip?" I inquired.

"It was more like a trek," replied the Wizard. "For most of us, life is no longer an adventure. It has become a habit—routine and predictable, and not very exciting. I need to trek periodically to step outside my regimen and renew my sense of aliveness."

"And that does it?" I asked with eyebrows raised.

"Like nothing else. A wilderness trek allows me to engage in and reflect upon challenging experiences. That is what life is all about—action and reflection. Most business managers and parents are long on action and short on reflection, yet it is the reflective side of life that gives meaning and purpose to the action. A trek enables you to test yourself and learn from the experience with undiluted, immediate, unforgiving feedback. You cannot con nature. Nature is not responsive to games and has no time for politics, nor does it respond to autocratic demands. In short, the challenge of nature gets you out of your comfort zone and helps you break through your self-imposed limitations."

"It does all that?" I asked incredulously.

"And more," said the Wizard. "There is nothing like nature to sort out your priorities. Life is very elemental, but we complicate it so. The natural world puts life back into perspective. That was why I advocated canoeing, if you recall. We need nature to activate our sense of wonder and to evoke our latent humility."

"Humility," I repeated. "That's where we left off last time. Let me tell you, it really threw me for a while. Humility sounded so wimpish, but I promised myself I would be open to new meanings."

"That is wise, for you will come to appreciate humility's awesome power," the Wizard asserted, peering over the top of his glasses.

"The awesome power of humility?"

"Absolutely. Humility is the key to breaking the ego barrier. It is the dragon slayer. Like the blind men from Indostan, if you have blind convictions that you are always right, you are not open to others. Your fixed opinions are mindsets that prevent choice and lock you into only one interpretation. There can be no creativity, no co-mingling of ideas and energies among people when you are not open. Without it, you will miss countless *how-to-be* opportunities. Humility is a centering act."

"But how do I practice humility?" I asked.

"Commune with nature. Observe a child at play. Contemplate a light year. Give—"

"A light year?" I interrupted.

"Yes. Have you ever really paused to think about a light year? It is the distance light travels in one year. This is the standard measurement for outer space, the cosmic equivalent to our earth-bound mile. Light travels at 186,000 miles per second. One light year is 5.88 trillion miles. That is 5.88 thousand, thousand, thousand, thousand miles! When I realize that the nearest star is 4.3 light years away, or 25 trillion miles, I feel a deep sense of humility. This grows when I realize the Hubble space telescope can see stars 14 billion light years away! How many miles is 5.88 trillion times 14 billion?"

"It puts things into perspective. . . ."

"In working with people," the Wizard shifted to his practical mode, "I recommend two preconditions for humility: First, you simply set aside your fixed opinions so that they do not block the exchange of ideas and energies; and second, you accept the other person unconditionally as having worth and being capable of contributing. This is an operational definition of humility."

"Simply said is not simply done," I asserted, recalling the Wizard's repeated claim that simple is not easy.

"I have said that ego pride is a manager's biggest problem," stated the Wizard, "whether you are managing a business or simply yourself. Historically, ego pride has been labeled the cardinal sin. If so, then humility is the cardinal virtue."

"You're sounding rather pious," I joked.

"I am only being practical. How can you or anyone else get the blinders off and see the whole elephant? We have such an adversary tradition in the West that we often fail to see how opposites complement each other. We think of light and darkness only as opposites, but if we look at the whole, they complement each other. Jung said, 'Light has need of darkness otherwise how could it appear as light?' In the absence of darkness, light has no meaning. It is death that makes life precious. Without evil, what would be the meaning of goodness? If we accept pride, we must also have humility."

I glanced, distracted, at those darker patches of brown on the backs of my hands and wondered if they too were pre-cancerous. They looked like benign "liver spots," so common with aging skin, but now I had reason to doubt—and doubt is corrosive to healing.

"Are you saying that when I have differences with another person, that I shouldn't look at the conflicting points of view?"

The Wizard turned to the photos on the table and selected a variety of shots—pictures of wild flowers, colorful lichen, rock faces, moss and incense cedar bark, conifer seedlings, mountain streams and water ouzels, sapsuckers and Coulter pinecones, and gray squirrels and Stellar jays. After I had looked at each picture, the Wizard handed me a broad panorama shot of the whole wilderness area, taken with a wide-angle lens.

"In nature, everything is different, yet each different piece fits into the larger scheme of things. And it works wonderful-ly well. When you change just one element in an ecosystem, all the other elements are affected. As such, the differences between these diverse elements can only be understood in the context of the whole. When you look at the big picture, you will learn to value differences. Two of your business col-leagues may argue from different positions, but in the larger context, they both want what is best for your company. Your family too is made up of very different individuals with dif-fering needs and perceptions but in a larger context, be it the family or the larger social order, they are all working toward the same end. This shared perception gives a new slant to everyone's differences."

"It all sounds good," I agreed, "but how can I embrace the whole when I have genuine differences with others?"

"Accept the differences, but focus on what you have in common rather than what separates you. The secret lies in where you put your attention. Nature has no problem accept-ing different species in the harmony of the whole. Focusing on differences is the curse of consciousness."

"And then humility, which is a centering act," I continued, "opens me up to other possibilities."

"You said it better than I," replied the Wizard, radiating with a sense of pleasure. "If you take a narrow perspective, you will limit your possibilities. Humility enlarges your frame of reference, which makes it easier to see all possibilities. Humility is the beginner's mind. Einstein had humility because he had a beginner's mind. With it, he could see the world as no one else had ever seen it before. The result was his tradition-shattering Theory of Relativity. Einstein was a beginner, totally unencumbered by 250 years of classical, scientific tradition. It takes strength, self-confidence, courage, and trust to open yourself to new possibilities—especially if they fly in the face of conventional wisdom.

"Your ego cannot control intuition, and it has no interest in things it cannot control. The result is a loss of intuition. That loss is too high a price to pay for control. You must learn what to control and what to allow. Life is a balance between the two."

"We're taught to control. It's very hard just to allow things to happen." I shrugged. I thought about the possible progression of my cancer and the vigil I had kept over my staff at work.

"The ego does not like to allow," declared the Wizard, "yet creativity is an allowing process. You cannot control the outcome of the creative process. If you try to control its outcome, you will lose the benefits that you seek. Creativity comes with intuition, not with analysis and reason. To gain control of the creative process, you will have to surrender yourself to intuition. Your ego does not understand that.

"Surrendering to intuition is risky, but risk does have its rewards. Your five senses detect only a very limited portion of what *is*. Without intuition as a sixth sense, you would have a very incomplete understanding of what *is*."

"There's that magic word again—*is*." I lighted up as if I'd just seen an old friend. "I recall you saying intuition gives us access to what *is*."

"What *is* is the truth, and intuition helps you access it. Everyone is naturally intuitive, but you and most other people don't know it because your conscious mind distracts you.

Your awareness increases when you quiet the noises of your conscious mind. This is the power of centering—the power of prayer, meditation, or just plain solitude. It is in these quiet moments that the truth is most likely to reveal itself, as in Major Keeble's saga.

"Intuition also tends to happen when it is least expected. After a long and passionate pursuit, having exhausted your conscious powers, you put your thoughts on the back burner. Later, in some trivial pursuit you get a flash of insight revealing answers that have eluded you in your most intense moments of rational inquiry. You need humility to allow intuition to do its work. It is a vital component to the development of the 'doctor within.' "

"The ego has difficulty with the 'doctor within,' " I spoke from experience.

"It does indeed, as the ego often cannot deal with the truth. The ego is not willing to share its turf with the doctor. Together, they could have the power of the whole."

"It's elephantine power—the power of the tusk, the trunk, and all the other parts working together," I cried exuberantly.

"Exactly," said the Wizard. "The whole is always more than the sum of its parts. In business management you often neglect the parts that cannot be measured. How do you measure staff commitment, will, spirit, purpose, teamwork, and inspiration? Is it fair to say that they do not count merely because they cannot be counted?

"Can you imagine how much better managers' decisions would be if they could see the larger whole within which they functioned? What if local decisions could be made with global considerations? The bigger your vision, the less parochial will be your decisions. The bigger the whole within you, the more capacity you will have to accommodate differences."

"Can you give me an example?"

The Wizard dug through his files and removed a dog-eared manila folder. He took a small piece of paper from it and handed it to me.

It read, "I have nothing, and yet I have everything—because I have God."

It was signed: Mother Teresa.

"Where did you get this?" I asked, completely awestruck.

"From her."

I sat motionless, transfixed by the written words before me. "Where did you meet her?"

"On a flight from London to Calcutta," said the Wizard. "Mother Teresa's capacity to love is so great, she can accommodate all the world's poor. The bigger the whole within us, the more capacity we have to accommodate differences. This is the essence of tolerance. 'Bigger' people are consistently able to rise above petty differences because they are more centered and they see the larger, longer-term considerations.

"I will give you another example. The demise of communism in Eastern Europe is evidence of the power of common human longings over an imposed ideology. In his famous speech at American University, President Kennedy said, 'Our most basic common link is that we all inhabit this small planet. We all breathe the same air. We all cherish our children's future. And we are all mortal.' That is a lovely statement of our shared commonality. If you have this truth within you, then you can absorb a lot of differences."

"Let me see if I got it. You say that truly big people are those who have a great capacity to accommodate differences because they see commonality in the larger context. And the larger the context, the smaller the differences appear to be. You're also saying that this larger context comes in part from being open to others—and this you call humility."

"Bravo!" applauded the Wizard. "This is the creative process in human interaction. It is *how to be* in life. As with all creative endeavors, the outcome is unknown—and therein lies the risk. You have to trust yourself and others to allow the creative process to happen. It is a risk because you are vulnerable. You might not get your way in the outcome. You will, however, be more likely to get an outcome that will satisfy all parties. And you will never know what other possibilities exist until you open yourself to the change process. That is humility."

"I like that—opening myself to the change process," I said.

"Earlier, you told me that the role of the doctor was to open the patient to healing. The role of the teacher then is to open the student to learning. And all this is just being open to change, right?"

"It is indeed," granted the Wizard. "Life is change, and change is the creative process. You cannot change until you open yourself to the forces of renewal within. Humility makes this possible. You recall the first time we met, I said you have access to all the power you need within you now. When you discover it, you will have your answers.

"Mother Teresa calls this power 'God.' Havel refers to the 'higher imperative' mediated to him by his conscience. Call it what you will, it is the *ultimate whole,* the totality within which all can be assimilated. Just as water is called the universal solvent of matter, you could say your higher imperative is the universal solvent in the domain of the spirit . . . ah, I fear I have gotten a bit ahead of myself."

"You've gotten a bit theoretical," I observed.

"Then I think I will change from metaphysics to mathematics. If you wish to add mixed fractions, you have to find a common denominator. For example, you cannot add 1/2 and 1/3 until you have enlarged the denominator to six, a number common to two and three. Then 1/2 becomes 3/6 and 1/3 becomes 2/6, making a sum of 5/6. Analogously, humility is your universal common denominator. It provides a larger whole for you to assimilate differences and integrate them into a newer, larger, and more creative whole."

"I use the term 'common denominator' all the time in resolving disputes, but as always, you put a new twist on the expression," I said admiringly.

"Humility exposes you to our common humanity—the qualities of joy, love, courage, humor, and truth. Have you ever known a person with true humility?" the Wizard asked. "You can literally feel the presence of all these qualities. They are palpable. We are talking about universal qualities, qualities of spirit that are understood and valued everywhere. With true humility, the 'doctor within' has a global practice."

I leaned over the table and grabbed the Wizard's hand. "So

you're saying that humility reveals what is—the truth, the essence of what I am. And that has universal appeal!"

"Humility reveals the commonality you share with all other people. It is a common bond of being that transcends language and ethnic differences. Right now, this common bond is obscured by different languages, customs and beliefs, and by the physical differences of size, shape, age, color, and sex. Given these explicit and visible differences, if you wish to find commonality, you must pay more attention to what is implicit about life, the invisible world of the spirit. This is the realm of a true leader. And that is the way life is."

Suggestions

Continue with your progress, as I attempted to after my meeting with the Wizard:

- The next time you meet someone with whom you have had differences, keep in mind being open to change . . . and be conscious of the two preconditions for humility:

  (a) Set aside your fixed opinions. Clear your mind of any expectations, predispositions, assumptions, or biases you might have. Make no judgments. Listen with a "beginner's mind," as if you had everything to learn.

  (b) Accept the other person unconditionally as having worth and being capable of making a contribution to the whole. Look for commonality and focus on this, accepting the differences that exist or looking for ways that the differences might co-exist in a larger context, a greater common denominator.

- You may need to see your relationship with this person from a longer time perspective. Be conscious of any fixed opinions you may have that might block the exchange of ideas and energy.

- Record your feelings and concerns with this "humility process." Assess the outcome in the fullest sense. See if this encounter suggests new thoughts or directions from you or the other party that were not present before—ideas that might be more mutually agreeable and satisfying. Assess your conclusions not just in the traditional sense of results, but look for qualitative changes in your relationship with the other person—attitudes, energy level, behavioral differences, and so on.

12
Quality Leadership

Leadership mobilizes the spirit of people.
Its essence is spiritual.

The more I thought about it and the more I practiced it, I could see the power of humility. It was the foundation for openness, trust, renewal, creative interaction, change, and developing the "doctor within." It was also a prerequisite for the "beginner's mind." The gift of human consciousness, the inherent wisdom of the unconscious mind, and the pure common essence of *how to be*—all of these are related to humility.

I had read about cancer patients who considered their disease a gift because it woke them up to an appreciation of life. The Wizard and his message were my gift, but the cancer scare had also added to my appreciation of good health and the healing power of family and friends. I developed a growing sense of humility for the profound gift of life itself.

I thought about my last session with the Wizard: "I am not aware of anything unless it passes through my consciousness. Here, the ego holds sovereign sway. As with all CEOs, there are forces, like the unconscious mind, that the ego cannot control. Intuition is my window on the unconscious mind. The ego cannot summon intuition on demand, but in true bureaucratic fashion, the ego can thwart it. It can keep intuition from my awareness. This is why the ego-dragon needs a periodic bashing. It needs to learn the fine art of allowing.

"The power of humility seems to lie in its ability to reveal my true self, the *is,* that is so much a part of the Wizard's teachings. The true self is our common humanity. It is obscured, however, by our explicit differences—our languages, skin colors, customs, and creeds. For this reason, I must pay more attention to the implicit in life, the realm of the true leader." The Wizard had talked about the differences between managers and leaders before, but it appeared he wanted to take it a step further.

When I first sought out the Wizard, I found myself wanting in life. Overcome with health, family, and business worries, I tried everything I could to control my life. By becoming a "possibility seeker" some months ago, I added a whole new dimension to my problem-solving approach to life. I was also trying to be a leader as well as a manager with new insights on *how to be.*

When we met again, the Wizard was behind his house playing with his basset hound. He was the first to speak. "Everybody needs a basset hound. They are great stress reducers. One look at her, and all your concerns vanish."

We enjoyed a good laugh together. "I thought you were going to say that if she is that ugly and not worried, what possible concerns can we have?"

With his eyebrows raised and a smile on his face, the Wizard pointed to me and said, "Beauty, is in the eye of the beholder. That statement says more about you than it does about her."

"Perhaps you're right."

"You left last time with a lot to think about. Is your life any different than it was before?"

Throwing up my arms in mock helplessness, I replied, "You tell me! You seem to know more about me than I do. I've had enough trouble coping with the visible world. Now you've got me worried about the invisible world, too!"

"Not to worry. It is all very natural," reassured the Wizard. "I merely suggested that you might pay more attention to the unseen."

"Why?" I asked, in my most childlike manner.

The Wizard paused, lowered his eyes, and stared momentarily at his hound. "In school you were taught that the world was composed of matter and energy. Yet today we know that they are one. Matter is energy. Everything is energy, yet did you know than nobody has ever seen pure energy? We only see the effects of it. One of its effects is matter. Matter is dense, visible energy. Your five senses make you aware of it. For most of us, matter is the only real world—it is the tangible, the visible, and the quantitative. The late David Bohm, a London physicist, called matter 'explicit energy.' In the explicit world, only matter really matters."

"Only matter matters?"

"Yes. The expression, 'It matters,' means that something is important; whereas, 'It doesn't matter,' means it is not important. In other words, non-matter is non-important. It is no wonder that our society has paid so little attention to the unseen world of energy. Our language has done us a great disservice."

"I hadn't thought of it that way."

"Few people do, but it is time we paid more attention to non-matter. David Bohm called this 'implicit energy,' the unseen counterpart of explicit energy. It is intangible, invisible, and qualitative, and it does not diminish with use or with time. When we spend it, our energy reservoir is not lessened for having done so. If anything, our energy is enhanced and others are energized, too."

"What do you mean by that?"

"If you share your happiness with another, are you the lesser for having done so? Is not the total sum of happiness greater in you and in others because of the expenditure? When you give inspiration to others, are you diminished by the amount that flows out of you?

"When I met Mother Teresa, I was instantly struck with the contrast between her frail, weathered body and the power of her presence. Physically, she was an old woman, but the intensity and strength of her spirit lifted me. It was palpable.

"Once again, there is a language problem here. Our society has no commonly accepted vocabulary for implicit energy.

Harrison Owen has written an excellent book, *Spirit*, on this very subject. Call it what you may—implicit, unseen, qualitative energy—it is simply *spirit*."

"Can you give me a for-instance?"

"Qualitative energy, or spirit, is a state of being. Spirit is what *is*. It is what makes us one with all people. We associate it with our related humanness, with feelings like love, courage, hope, joy, laughter, and compassion. And spirit need not diminish with time. Contrast spirit with physical energy, which peaks around age twenty and then diminishes at the rate of about one percent per year. Physically, you are a diminishing asset. Spiritually, you have growth potential. Now you are a businessperson concerned with growth and the preservation of assets. Where will you put your money?"

"That's a provocative question."

"I hope so," said the Wizard earnestly. "You have to provoke in order to attract attention to the unseen. In the competition for the hearts and minds of human beings, it is hard to compete with the material world. Matter exerts a powerful pull on our senses. We are just trying to get equal time for spirit."

"But how can we compete?"

The Wizard invited me to walk with him. The hound led the way, her head held high, tail arcing up proudly behind, and stumpy legs padding briskly along. The Wizard, deep in reflection, said nothing. I no longer felt awkward with the Wizard's silent times. Suddenly, the basset hound stopped, catching a scent. With her ears uplifted, her nose searched the air for the scent. Then, as quickly as she had stopped, she lowered her nose to the ground and set off into the woods, barking excitedly. Moments later, she circled back to pick up the scent she had temporarily lost. Once again, her barking grew fainter as she disappeared into the woods. The Wizard paused to watch this ritual.

"Rabbit," he explained to me. Then he started to think outloud about my question. "You asked me how spirit can compete with the world of the senses. The short answer is, with concentration, with focusing your attention, with awareness.

Normally your awareness is captured by the sights and sounds outside of you or by your internal emotional reactions, such as fears or worries. You have just witnessed a classic demonstration of this. When my hound, Alphie, catches a scent, it does not matter what was on her mind the moment before. That is history! She is now totally captivated by the rabbit's scent. Her keen sense of smell regulates her life."

"But Alphie's response enables her to survive," I argued. "It isn't bad to respond to what's around you. You have to respond to the outside world, of course."

"Yes, but life for humans is more than just survival," said the Wizard. "Alphie has no choice but to follow her nose. You, however, do have choice. You do not have to follow the 'scent' wherever it goes. You have the capacity to direct your awareness to matters of your choice. Awareness takes you out of this servitude to your senses and gives you the freedom to choose. It is really the self asserting control over the senses— like a master with his hound, telling it to be still on command or sending it out on a task."

"So the issue is really control," I inferred. "Am I in charge of my mind or do I allow it to go undisciplined randomly, reacting to the scent of the moment?"

"I think you have put your finger on the key—discipline," said the Wizard. "The problem of losing focus of spirit is due to the unwarranted intervention of external distractions and random thoughts. These distractions fragment you and break your concentration. You will want to be able to shut out these distractions, if you choose to do so, yet remain totally aware of everything around you. That is true concentration, the state of relaxed awareness, that we talked about earlier. If you allow your thinking process to wander around unchecked, then you will be unable to access the full power of your being."

"I've always believed that thinking and reasoning are what distinguishes us from lower forms of life," I said.

"It is true that our intellectual capacity is more highly evolved than other known forms of life, but you are presupposing that we are at the top of the great Chain of Being. Not so," declared the Wizard. "There are higher forms of life that we are not capable of understanding. Thus, faith and intuition are higher powers than thinking and reasoning."

"I see where you're coming from, Wizard. If I simply respond to stimuli, then I'm a basset hound. I want to be able to choose to 'follow my nose' rather than having my nose do all the choosing for me."

"Well said."

"Thanks. I'm reminded of our 'urgent and important' discussion a while ago. It sounds very familiar. The hound is a slave to the urgent."

"She is enthralled and enslaved with what is urgent outside of her," said the Wizard. "The issue is how to achieve a balance in your life. In physics, they call it *equipoise* or *equilibrium*. There is no denying the material world's powerful pull on our senses."

"You said you wanted equal time for spirit," I recalled.

"Our society once had it, but sadly we have been demythologized. The basic theme of all mythology is an invisible or spirit world supporting the visible. The two worlds are inseparable, but we fail to 'see' the spirit. In all of us, the visible and the invisible act as one, each working its magic on the other. Our physical energy provides a fit, vital, healthy, relaxed body for the spirit. At the same time, spirit offers purpose, meaning, hope, and direction to the body." As the Wizard spoke, he cupped his hands to form a sphere. "Together they make a whole."

"I fear I'm way out of balance. There's no equipoise here!" I admitted. "With my cancer scare, I've been overconcerned with the physical."

"That is the norm," assured the Wizard, "but the good news is that if we admire the qualities of spirit and desire to have them ourselves, then we will move in the direction of spirit. You literally can 'absorb' from others the qualities you desire. The mental image that we desire evokes the associated feelings and actions that bring it about. See yourself as a certain kind of person, and then you will act as if it were so. There is no reason not to have a balance, if you desire it."

"Then you're saying that we become more like those we admire?"

"That is right," said the Wizard. "That is the power of leadership."

"What do you mean?" I asked, knowing the Wizard would put a different slant on things.

"Leadership mobilizes the spirit of people. Its essence is spirit. Once again, however, language disadvantages us. For example, when ideas become tangible actions, we say they *materialize*. When leaders raise the spirit of people with purpose and inspiration, however, we do not say they *spiritualize* them. Yet, that is exactly what happens. Managers mobilize material resources. In doing so, they materialize an organization. They monitor the quantitative side of business. Leaders, as opposed to mere managers, mobilize spirit. As such, they spiritualize an organization. Their realm is the qualitative side of business. Quality is the business of leadership."

"Quality and leadership are vital issues today, but I hadn't made that direct connection."

"Much has been written about the difference between managers and leaders. I have now expressed my opinion," said the Wizard. "The manager deals with the material, the leader with the spirit. If you are to achieve a balance in your life, you need to be both a manager and a leader. The management side, like the urgent, prevails because it is quantitative. It is measurable, so you can get a handle on it. The leadership side gets neglected because it is abstract and elusive.

"This is the point: If you do not attend to the qualities of the human spirit, the quality of your products and services will suffer. Quality begins with the quality of human energy expended on your products and services."

"You're saying it's not the product or the service but the quality of the energy behind it all that counts," I paraphrased. "And with my children, it's not the time or the activities but the quality of energy I put into them. I suppose it's also not important to focus on my medical test results—it's the quality of the energy I put into my life and overall health that counts. Now that's a different way of viewing my life."

"You said it," approved the Wizard. "Our world cries out for attention to the qualitative dimension. This is why quality and leadership are so in demand. We have been deprived of quality because we have not acknowledged the seminal significance of the human spirit. The new frontier of quality begins with the invisible, intangible, qualitative dimensions of the human spirit: commitment, will, purpose, vision, love, and a host of others. The power of leadership grows when we share it because leaders potentiate people who release their energies and make things happen."

"And I always thought power came from control."

"It does for the manager, but not for the leader." The Wizard's manner grew more intense. "This is a very important distinction. Management power comes from *controlling* material resources. Leadership power comes from *releasing* human resources. It follows then that quality improvement starts with human considerations. This is how quality is built into a product, a service, or a relationship."

"What you're saying, Wizard, is that we build quality by building the people. That's what you called 'getting people done through work.' "

"Exactly," applauded the Wizard. "Regrettably, our society is obsessed with numbers. Managers have to make their numbers, but when the numbers become the raison d'être, the reason for being, a business loses its qualitative edge. It literally loses its spirit. What we fail to realize is that numbers are important only as measures, and they are inadequate at best. What is vital is the human energy expended to meet those numbers. Athletes know that the numbers will follow if they pursue a comprehensive training regimen that addresses the whole person— body, mind, and spirit. What works in athletic achievement holds true for business, as well."

"You're saying 'making the numbers' is important, but when it becomes my purpose, I lose sight of the human spirit, the source of those numbers?"

"Yes, and what is more," added the Wizard, "numbers are not leading indicators of how a business is doing. They are the tangible, trailing indicators. The numbers merely confirm.

They quantify what has already happened. The leading indicators are all based in spirit—like hope, optimism, confidence, and courage. These are also the leading indicators of the stock market."

"Somebody once said that managing a business by the numbers is like driving a car by looking in the rear-view mirror."

"That is an apt metaphor," said the Wizard. "You simply have to attend to the spirit if you want to be out front. There is a quantitative fixation that more is better. This is what E. F. Schumacher, author of *Small is Beautiful,* had in mind when he said, 'The whole point is to give the idea of growth a qualitative determination.' Growth is not just more. Growth with a qualitative determination lifts, enhances, and ennobles the human spirit."

"That's what we call *quality of life.*"

"Yes, although there is some confusion there. Many who complain about a declining quality of life equate it with less purchasing power or a decrease in their standard of living. Most often, this refers to quantity of life. True quality of life has little to do with these measures. Most of us need a better balance, however. To achieve this, we need to remember that spirit gives life to matter. Therefore, spirit should be our first consideration."

"You're just saying I need to get my priorities right, but not neglect matter?" I looked to the Wizard for some confirmation on this.

"Of course. It is very hard to neglect matter, but it is easy to neglect spirit. That was my original point," said the Wizard. "Any way you look at the world—cosmologically, religiously, economically, historically—matter evolves from spirit. Spirit is the creative source, the producer. Matter is the product."

With that, the Wizard took a Swiss Army knife out of his pocket and handed it me. I turned it over in my hand, puzzled. "Why the knife?" I asked.

"Think of this knife as matter, crafted and sold by spirit. This product has a world-wide reputation for quality. What makes it so is the Swiss tradition of precision and craftsmanship embodied in hundreds of people who produce this product. Their loyalty, their dedication, their pride, their respect, their love—all this and much more goes into making this product what it is. If they did not feel this way about their product, their company, their co-workers, their customers and indeed, themselves, the product would lose this qualitative input, this infusion of spirit. And it would soon begin to show. So where does quality start?"

"You've made your point."

"The world is transforming in a very fundamental way," reflected the Wizard. "Matter is not what we once thought it was, and that realization is changing our material world. We think in metaphors, and as the metaphors of science change, our thinking changes with them.

"Intuitive people have always known that life is more than what we see. Without realizing it, we all extend far beyond the physical boundaries of our bodies and actively participate in the unseen world of spirit. This is the next frontier that we can explore at another time. That is the way life is."

Suggestions

The "invisible world"—as if the world of matter wasn't enough to deal with now! I tried to expand my focus to a whole other realm. Here are several things the Wizard suggested to help me to see how the seen and unseen interact in our everyday lives.

- List what you value in a relationship. (Have a specific person in mind for each of the following relationships.)

  With a family member
  With a friend
  With your manager
  With an employee
  With a customer

  1. How does this relate to quality of life? Are these things that you value tangible and material or intangible qualities of the spirit?

2. What conclusions do you draw from this about what you value in a person? In a relationship?

- Think about what makes a relationship deteriorate. Have a specific person in mind as in the above suggestion.

  1. Are the causes tangible and quantitative or intangible and qualitative?
  2. How does this impact your quality of life?

- When you are feeling tired or down, what picks you up? For example, it's early in the evening and you're sitting at home. You feel tired and you have nothing planned. The phone rings and a friend asks you out on the spur of the moment. It sounds inviting. Instantly, you feel energized. Your fatigue is gone.

  1. What was the source of that energy? A voice? An image in your mind?
  2. What sources you? What are your wellsprings of energy? Are they from within you or are they external to you?
  3. If external, can you create this same energy from within, with no outside intervention? How?

- Think about an experience you've had on the job or at home where everything went right for you, where you felt "on top of things"—a peak experience.

  1. Describe how you felt.
  2. What were the conditions (the nature) of the task or experience that made it feel like a peak experience? Are these qualitative conditions?
  3. How can you create more of these peak experiences at home or on the job? What changes will you have to make in yourself, your relationships, and your physical environment to add what Schumacher called "a qualitative determination to your life?

13
Creating Action at a Distance

We still have not grasped that matter is more than what we see.

I **continued** to be symptom-free of cancer. This was encouraging, but in my heart I knew it would be five years before I could say I was cured. Knowing that I could be symptomatic at any time caused me some anxiety, but I was determined not to feel victimized. Life was too rich for me to succumb to self-pity.

As always, after a visit with the Wizard, I had much to think about. The Wizard had taken the distinction between a manager and a leader a step further for me. He was now talking about spirit, or qualitative energy. I had never thought about this, but now I saw that spirit was always implicitly present. It's true, we don't give this the attention it deserves. What we see is explicit, but the Wizard said that this was only an outcome of spirit.

I had always been a number cruncher in business, and I thought I knew what it took to reach those numbers, but spirit has added a whole new dimension. Recently I had launched a quality program with an emphasis on products and processes. I now realized that these products were no better than the spirit that gave rise to them. The human spirit was truly the source of quality products. I concluded that I had done a reasonably good job with the material side of my business, but I had undervalued the human spirit of my associates—and myself, too. I was intrigued with the idea that leaders spiritualize an organization. I had already seen significant changes in the spirit of my staff as I changed my behavior. But I was the leader and I had a lot more work to do on myself. I also saw how the same principles extended to my personal life, my health, and my family. I longed for spirit to energize me in all areas of my life.

The Wizard had said matter is not what we thought it was and this realization is transforming our world in a very fundamental way. He also said we think in metaphors and as the metaphors of science change, our thinking changes with them. I wondered what he meant by this.

When we met the next time, it was late in the day. The sun was setting an hour earlier with daylight saving. The Wizard invited me to join him on a raised deck to witness this splendid nightly ritual.

"The early Egyptians believed that a goddess swallowed the sun in the west, allowed it to pass through her body for twelve hours, and then gave birth to it the following morning in the east." Smiling, the Wizard turned to me and said," I wish the subject of the evening were as simple as all that."

"I can handle a bit more complexity than that," I said laughingly, "but not much more!"

"Good. Where to begin?" The Wizard scratched his chin. "Until 1543 we thought that the sun revolved around the earth. Conventional wisdom supported this belief proposed by Ptolemy, the Greek astronomer, 1400 years earlier. After all, this finding could be confirmed with our own observations," said the Wizard, pointing to a half horizon-obscured sun.

"That year the great Polish astronomer Copernicus died and published posthumously that the earth revolved around the sun! He apparently didn't want to be alive for the storm of protests that inevitably followed. His theory reversed Ptolemy's belief that the earth was the center of the universe and had no motion.

"Nearly seventy years later Galileo confirmed the Copernican theory with his telescope discoveries. Many church officials opposed Galileo because his findings were contrary to the teachings of the church. They warned him to abandon the Copernican theory and they put Copernicus' book on their prohibited list where it remained for 200 years! In 1632 the Inquisition tried Galileo, forced him to recant his findings, and placed him under house arrest. New paradigm proponents are often not popular, let alone not believed. Nevertheless, a paradigm shift had begun."

"What's a paradigm?"

"Sorry, I should have explained. A paradigm is a common belief that is largely unquestioned. We accept it as real and live accordingly.

"Isn't it curious," he continued as the horizon enveloped the last luminous crescent of sun to reveal a deep orange 'Halloween' sky. "We still say 'sunset' and 'sunrise' as if it were so! It takes a long time—452 years since Copernicus proposed this disturbing truth—to assimilate knowledge that runs contrary to popular beliefs."

"It's like those habit patterns you talked about, isn't it?"

"Exactly," replied the Wizard. "Ambrose Bierce said, 'Habit is a shackle for the free.' We are shackled to our habits. Only this is much broader at the cultural level. Today there is a revolution in progress fueled by the findings of quantum physics. Its impact upon our lives is enormous. In its simplest form, it is an emerging realization of wholeness within which everything is dynamic and interrelated. Nothing stands alone."

"Tell me about these findings," I said, eager for more specifics.

"Traditional beliefs die hard as we have seen. Galileo's work formed the basis for Sir Isaac Newton's theories of a predictable, orderly, mechanistic universe that held sway for nearly 300 years. Newton's 'clockwork' universe theory made sense, and still does at the visible level; but it doesn't hold at the subatomic nor at the cosmic levels, which are integral and indivisible parts of the greater whole. As physicists searched for the ultimate 'building blocks' of existence, they came to a startling realization."

"Which was?"

"There are no building blocks."

"How can there be no building blocks?"

"It is the wrong metaphor," the Wizard asserted. "Remember, matter is energy. Newtonian theory held that matter was solid and indestructible. So, naturally, scientists looked for the ultimate source, the 'building blocks' of this solid matter. We now know that matter at the subatomic level is not a material substance. It only appears solid to our senses. Matter is mostly 'empty' space in which subatomic 'particles' randomly occur, move at incredible speeds, collide with one another to destroy themselves, and create new particles in the process. Unlike the orderly and predictable world of Newton, the universe is really a random, dynamic 'dance of energy.' If we think of 'building blocks', we cannot even comprehend quantum theory."

"If not building blocks, what then?"

"To comprehend this reality today our metaphors of thought must be more fluid, more organic, more holistic. Physicists now talk in terms of energy fields, waves, spin, velocity, and force-carrying particles. These are not suggestive of building blocks. A more appropriate metaphor is electromagnetic fields of energy."

"But aren't these particles solid?"

"Nobody has ever seen one, only their tracings in the bubble chamber of a particle accelerator. Furthermore, their location and movement cannot be predicted accurately. Physicists call this 'the uncertainty principle.' In the absence of certainties they must deal with statistical probabilities. And scientists are not comfortable with uncertainties.

"To make it even more puzzling," continued the Wizard, "particles are probably not particles at all, but momentary manifestations of interacting energy fields. In other words, particles are interfaces or interconnections among commingling energy fields."

"I'm afraid you've lost me," I said, throwing up my arms.

"I see why the building block theory persists. At least I can understand that!"

"You're not the first to be lost in the quantum maze," assured the Wizard. "The problem is that we have been taught to think in terms of parts and pieces and not the whole. The paradigm shift requires us to think more *holistically*."

"Can you give me an example?" I asked.

"In our daily lives we are always struggling to pull our lives together. Fragmentation is a way of life. The focus is on the pieces. We talk of 'getting our act together,' of 'tying up the loose ends,' of 'putting things into place,' and of 'getting in touch with ourselves.' All of these terms speak of our lives in pieces and they signal a quest for unity or wholeness. Life seems to be a journey of integration, a preoccupation with getting the pieces together."

"I can identify with this. That's why I'm here."

"With these common expressions we are defining the whole in terms of the sum of the parts. Quantum reality at the sub-atomic level is the other way around. The only way to understand the parts is first to grasp the larger context of the whole. This is what I called 'healing' when we first met. It is seeing the whole elephant first. Only then do the parts, like the tusk and the tail, make sense. For you, this starts with seeing yourself whole, visualizing yourself as a complete person, rather than looking at what parts of you need fixing."

"Ah, I see what you are saying," I responded excitedly. "We talked about this earlier with imagination and the power of possibilities."

"Yes, the focus must be on the whole for that is what *is*—a seamless web of dynamic energy patterns. Particles have no existence on their own. Nor do we. They have meaning only in relationship with the larger whole. As do we. We have to start with the whole to understand the parts. This is a different starting point for us, a whole new perception or, should I say, a new perception of the whole!" The Wizard smiled, pleased with his subtle turn of words.

"It's easier to see the fragments, isn't it?"

"This is the nature of our conscious, knowing mind, if you recall. It differentiates, separates one part from another. The problem we have with quantum theory is that we cannot picture it. Our conscious mind cannot grasp it"

"I remember the physics experiments in school," I interjected, "where the teacher illustrated Newton's laws with billiard balls. I can still picture those experiments very clearly. It made so much sense."

"Billiard balls are solid, visible, three-dimensional objects. It is hard to abandon something so tangible for subatomic activity that we cannot see and doesn't make sense. Remember, at the subatomic level those solid billiard balls are mostly 'empty' space."

"You're right. It doesn't make sense. It's nonsense to me."

"It is, quite literally, 'nonsense' when we view it from our limited three-dimensional, 'billiard-ball' reality. Classical science has always tried to preserve the objectivity of its findings by holding observers independent of their observations. The idea was that we could step back, observe something, and draw conclusions without affecting its outcome. We now know that this is not possible. The observer affects the observed! For example, light may appear as waves or as particles depending upon how the observer measures it. Physicists call this *complementarity,* a word that explains the complementary qualities of these two simultaneous states. Observation permits us to describe only one of these functions at a time, yet both exist. It doesn't make sense, but that is its nature.

"It does make sense, however, in the larger, space-time world that lies beyond our senses. That is the whole we have to grasp for the 'nonsense' to make sense. Scientists speculate on this unseen whole with theories which they try to prove or disprove. So far quantum theory has stood the test of time and rigorous scrutiny. What we see with our 'billiard-ball' eyes are only visible manifestations of a deeper, invisible, multi-dimensional reality. Unless we are willing to admit that this 'nonsense' exists, we cannot grasp the new reality."

"This is extraordinary—the ultimate reality is 'nonsense!' "

"I am afraid it is unless we make that quantum leap," affirmed the Wizard. "Classical theory held that matter existed independently in a void. Quantum theory, however, says matter is not independent because the void is not void, but alive with energy. We cannot separate matter from the fields of energy within and around it. That is a far cry from the billiard balls of classical thinking."

"I am more comfortable with the 'billiard ball' world."

"So were the inquisitors who persecuted Galileo."

I felt a little uncomfortable with the idea that I was in a class with the seventeenth-century inquisitors but I had to admit the principle was the same.

"This has been a long time coming," reflected the Wizard. "Newton's clockwork universe was a useful metaphor until we learned more about space and the nature of matter. In 1831 Michael Faraday, an English physicist and natural philosopher, discovered electromagnetic fields. Faraday proved there was more than nothingness in space. The significance of this finding over 160 years ago has not yet sunk into our consciousness. We still have not grasped that matter is more than what we see.

"The discovery of electromagnetic fields dealt the first blow to the classical theory of solid objects moving in a void. An electromagnetic field is a disturbance in the space around a charged body. Charged bodies create fields of energy in space that affect other charged bodies. Matter 'disturbs' the space around it. The presence of matter affects, and is affected by, the unseen energy fields about it."

"You're saying matter is energy and it is surrounded by fields of energy. In other words, everything is energy and it all sort of runs together."

"You're getting the hang of it," the Wizard said. "If we think of matter as energy vibrations, which it is, then it is easy to imagine energy fields emanating from matter. Rupert Sheldrake, a Cambridge trained biologist, defines matter as 'vibratory energy bounded by extended fields of energy.' "

The moon was hanging like a large clipped fingernail in the southern sky as the Wizard pointed to it. "Look at that, the earth's natural satellite, and be reminded that it moves our tides. At a mean distance of 238,857 miles from the earth, this relatively small celestial body 'disturbs' our oceans. Newton taught us that gravity in outer space 'disturbs' other celestial bodies.

"Now, quantum theory teaches us that particles in inner space also disturb the space around them such that other particles feel the force of their presence. Thus, the infinitely small particles of inner space and the huge bodies of outer space both have something in common."

"What's that?"

"They create what physicists call *action at a distance*. When the moon moves the tides, that is creating action at a distance. The same sort of phenomenon occurs at the subatomic level with particles. Parts do not operate independently in a void. They cannot be separated from the 'space,' or force fields, around them. In short, everything in inner space and outer space affects, and is affected by, everything else. Therefore, to understand any part of this interconnectedness, you have to start with the whole."

"So where does all this take us?"

"If this is so with matter at the most elemental and at the cosmic levels, would it not hold true for us in our lives as well? Are we not 'charged bodies' who extend far beyond the boundaries of our physical being? Are we not also capable of creating 'action at a distance?'

"Dr. Sheldrake maintains that memory is inherent in nature and therefore all species can learn, develop, and adapt through a process he calls *morphic resonance*. For example, after rats have learned a skill in one place, other rats elsewhere are more readily able to learn that skill. Nature stores the learning in 'morphic fields' that resonate to all like members of a species independent of space and time. Putting this in human terms, he would say the more people who learn how to use computers, the easier it should be for others to do so. The achievement of athletic records could indicate the presence of this force. If you accept this possibility, then Jung's theory of the collective unconscious is mainstream stuff! This is not only action at a distance, it is action across time as well."

"Wow! That's far out!"

"Sheldrake's theory helps us to understand the wisdom of the ages stored in our unconscious mind and available to us through intuition. It really is not so far out considering the evidence he presents. Contrasted with morphic resonance, to say "the observer affects the observed" is now pretty tame stuff! Remember, we do affect the outcome of what we observe. We disturb the reality we see."

"I know that if somebody is looking at me, I am affected by this."

"Ah," said the Wizard, "but quantum theory says observers disturb us even if we are not aware of their presence! Observers are not passive. They actively participate in the outcome of what they observe.

"We have said there is power in focusing attention, power in concentration. When you direct your attention to another person, it has consequences. Managers have known since the famous Hawthorne studies in the 1930's that attention raised workers' productivity.

"A half century later we can take this a quantum step further. A 1988 study of a coronary care group verified the healing power of intercessory prayer. It revealed that the 'prayed for' members needed considerably less acute medical care than the others. To pray for another is to disturb the outcome. That is creating action at a distance."

"That's amazing. You said in an earlier meeting that our reality, our truth, is what we perceive. So then, if observers affect what they observe, are they not in effect creating their own reality?"

"They are not solely responsible for creating their own reality. Think of observers as cocreators," affirmed the Wizard, "along with everything else. Conscious, caring attention has the power to change outcomes."

"Its almost spooky, when you think about it," I said. "On the other hand, if everything connects to everything else, it makes sense. Disturb a piece of it and in some way you disturb the rest. As you said some time ago, this is just like making changes in an ecosystem. Change one element, and you alter the whole system. It occurs to me that sages have been saying this for centuries, so really what's new?"

"The fact that sages and scientists are saying the same things is what is new. Today, the line between physicists and philosophers blurs. This is the paradigm shift—the realization of our connectedness. This perception spells an end to dualism, the separation of spirit and matter which began with the age of science.

"Western civilization built its foundations on science, which separated matter from spirit and focused its energy on the former. Science, the very discipline that split the two worlds, now points to their unity, a victim of its own pursuit. Science must now deal with spirit, the very thing that originally lay outside its purview."

"And so," I concluded, "modern physics isn't saying anything new, just confirming ancient wisdom."

"Science is validating what sages have long known. The scientific method requires that we understand the parts in order that we may grasp the whole. Quantum theory claims that we cannot understand the parts except in the context of the whole. First, we have to imagine the whole in order for the parts to make sense. It is a complete shift of perception. The new physics is making us think more holistically."

"And you think this affects us in our everyday lives?"

"Yes, I do. You see, we think in metaphors. 'Building blocks' are no longer adequate to explain the realities today. Electromagnetic fields, force fields of energy, are more appropriate metaphors now. These are very different mental models from building blocks and they require profound shifts in our thinking from tangible and visible things to intangible and invisible forces."

"So," I summarized, "in accepting this new invisible reality, we change the way we think about things."

"That's right. That is the paradigm shift. One physicist contends that matter 'died' with the birth of classical science 300 years ago. The universe was believed to be a giant mechanism composed of inert parts that moved to the dictates of immutable laws. This shift in our thinking gives new life to the natural world as we become more aware of our connections with it. The dance of energy is changing our lives."

"Can you say more about how this might change my life?

"This is very significant. When we fully understand this shift, we will no longer fear change."

"I don't get the connection."

"So long as we see matter as solid, unchanging reality, then change equates to losing something. That is, any change in our present condition is a loss of something familiar to us. Therefore, we tend to resist change. Whereas, if we accept matter as a constantly changing dance of energy, then change *is* reality and we can accept that 'loss' as natural, even desirable. Reality is not fixed solid matter, but ever-moving energy, a creative evolutionary process. The universe is abundantly creative, always giving us something new and different. Life is change and change is what *is*. Rather than fearing the loss of something that we possess, we can look forward to a continuously evolving reality—one that is new at every moment. To resist change, therefore, is to resist life! To embrace change is to embrace life! This is a shift of enormous magnitude."

"I wouldn't want it said that I resist life, but . . ."

"Then open your heart to change. The other aspect of this shift is a renewed appreciation of the invisible. I have said the new physics has opened our awareness to the whole and to the dynamic nature of matter. It also calls our attention to the unseen, the deeper reality that lies in and around the world we see. Intuitive people have always known that we are more than what we see, that we extend far beyond the boundaries of our bodies."

"Those are the energy fields of our 'charged bodies' right?"

"Certainly. Eastern thought has long recognized the presence of extra-corporeal energy in the form of auras, chakras, and meridians in what is known as the subtle body. Spiritual healing, even distance healing, is not uncommon today, yet classical theory conditions us to think otherwise. The new physics helps us to understand the limitless possibilities beyond our five senses. It enables us to see how we participate in the unseen world of energy. The impact we have on the space about us is just beginning to be realized. It is truly magical."

"Magical?"

"Yes. We have always associated magic with the powers of the unseen. As Leonard Sweet said in *Quantum Spirituality*, 'God leaves more fingerprints than blueprints . . . magic, in its deepest, truest sense, means the presence of the infinite in the finite, the eternal in the mortal, the wondrous in the common.'"

"That's a lovely thought. With the renaissance of the invisible perhaps we can expect a rebirth of magic."

"We have always had magical powers. We have just lost the belief in them. That was one of the casualties of classical science with its need for proof. A child's world is very magical, but this is short lived. Imagination and creativity are soon educated out of children. Fortunately the dance of energy, the creative evolutionary process, has restored the magic to matter."

"I recall reading something about the earth being a living thing. Is this what you mean?"

"Precisely. You are probably referring to the work of James Lovelock, the leading proponent of the *Gaia* hypothesis, the idea that the earth is a living organism."

"It doesn't seem as far-fetched now in light of what you've said. When I was in school we learned the difference between animate, or living things, and inanimate things, like rocks. If the earth is alive, it sounds like that difference is now in question."

"Good point. At the subatomic level these distinctions make no sense. It is all energy and it is all moving. So what is alive and what isn't?"

"Sounds like it's all alive."

"That's the dance of energy, the magic of matter."

"'Nonsense' is beginning to make sense," I said with some relief.

"For most of us reality is the world of our senses, limited largely to what we can see, hear, and touch. This is so limiting and, paradoxically, so unreal. We live seemingly content with only what we see, but our lives are largely shaped by what we don't see.

"Ironic, is it not?" The Wizard smiled. "Business, the ultimate material enterprise, is being forced to acknowledge spirit with its life-giving essence. Spirit, by nature, comes first. When you attend to spirit first, you enhance the quality of your life and you begin to see the larger context, the interconnectedness of life. Putting spirit first is being human, and being human is simply what we are. That is the way life is."

Suggestions

The Wizard challenged me with a series of exercises to illustrate our oneness:

1. We live in an interdependent world. The flow of water, gas, electricity, electronic messages, goods and services keep our lives going. Any interruption of this flow in our post-modern, interdependent world causes dislocations in our lives. These disruptions may be mere inconveniences or disasters.

   • The same is true in the ecosystems of our natural world. Take a moment to sense the interrelationships and the interconnections of the fauna and flora about you. Begin by focusing on a specific species of animal, flower, tree, bird, or insect in your immediate environment. Carefully observe the context in which it lives. Sense its interdependency on all the natural elements in the web of relationships that form its habitat. Imagine what dislocations occur when we alter its environment. Think in terms of dislocations in your area caused by new roads, home-building, land-clearing, development of farmland, cutting trees, draining wetlands, adding road salt, spraying pesticides, applying chemical fertilizers, topsoil erosion, lake and stream pollution, air quality changes, and so on. The idea is not to think of global patterns such as acid rain and greenhouse gas build-up, but to keep it local. And observe and imagine what changes these factors cause to a specific animal, bird, insect, or plant.

2. Now do the same with yourself. Sense the intricate and fragile pattern of relationships that sustains you with your land, your home, your pets and belongings, your family and close friends, your work and community acquaintances. Sense the illusion of independence and the reality of interdependence.

Then extend that pattern to the larger society, to the state in which you live, and to the country as a whole. Sense how social, political, and economic decisions made at these levels affect you. More important, sense how everything you do, in some small way, also affects the social, political, and economic conditions of the larger unit.

Now extend that web of interconnectedness to the world and feel the impact of global decisions on your life and vice versa.

Finally extend the web to the moon, the sun and its other planets. Know that if the moon can lift the seas of the earth with its gravitational pull, it is doing something to you as well. Know too that if the sun can blind and blister you at a distance of 93 million miles, it does unseen things as well. Know too that the lifestyle you choose in some way disturbs or impacts the effect these cosmic forces have on you.

3. Imagine you are taking a trip inside yourself. First at the gross anatomical level of your blood vessels, muscles, bones, and organs.

Then move more deeply imaginatively into your cells, into your DNA, the genetic code that determines who and what you are, and its intertwined double helix of genes and chromosomes.

Now move even more deeply into the atoms with their protons and electrons orbiting about their nuclei like miniature solar systems.

Finally move into the quantum world of subatomic particles, the dance of energy in an immense void. Sense the mystery, the interconnectedness, the web of relationships at all levels. Be aware of the gradual progression from mass and matter to energy and the void of 'inner' space.

4. Assume that your energy extends far beyond your physical body and that you are able to create action at a distance with the power and energy you possess now. Care for another person in your life by focusing loving thoughts, or prayers on that person. Observe the effects over time on the other person, on you, and on the relationship.

Extend that field of loving care to practice "distant healing" on someone outside your immediate world. Believe in its power and know that it is having an impact even if it is not observable.

14

From the Head to the Heart

*What counts is the spirit, the quality of being,
that I bring to the act of doing.*

I **was** still a bit bewildered by our last meeting, although I took some solace in his saying I was not the first to be lost in the quantum maze. The Wizard said the world was changing in a very fundamental way that involves our understanding of the nature of matter. Apparently the Newtonian concept of an orderly mechanical universe is not the way it is at the subatomic and cosmic levels. What we see is not the ultimate reality. Matter is not solid. Newton, of course, had no way of knowing this. The Wizard said we have to think in terms of invisible energy fields and that everything is moving in a seemingly random manner that defies prediction and leaves us with uncertainties. Obviously we need to develop an appreciation for the unseen.

I recalled from my college physics class that we could only see a very narrow range of the electromagnetic spectrum. Our eyes were limited to the seven rainbow colors from red to violet. After all, we can't see ultra-violet or infra-red waves at either end of the spectrum. Nor can we see radio waves or x-rays and a whole host of others. So perhaps it should not be so surprising that the ultimate reality lies beyond our senses, perhaps even beyond our comprehension. If matter is "energy bounded by fields of energy," the so-called void must be an incomprehensible "soup" of interacting energy fields. In this context, I could see how everything is in some way connected to everything else.

One of the most provocative things the Wizard said was that we human beings extend far beyond the boundaries of our bodies. We are inseparably linked to all about us. This unseen world was the next frontier for managers. When we met again, the Wizard was in his back yard. I asked him about Alphie.

"Oh, she is out terrorizing the rabbit world," he said. "In truth, she has never caught one yet, but that does not seem to bother her. It is the chase that excites. There is a lesson there in passion, pursuit, and persistence."

"My passion and pursuit, I fear, have been largely misdirected. I have undervalued spirit. As such, I haven't been much of a leader."

"You are being too tough on yourself," consoled the Wizard. "Few of us qualify on that count. But let me share some more thoughts on the subject.

"Qualitative energy, or spirit, can only be experienced. This is the function of art. Artists capture the ineffable qualities of life through the media of sound, color, or movement. This is the realm of music, art, and dance. They touch our being. Poets are celebrated for their power to evoke with word imagery the feeling of the experience itself. Storytellers have historically connected one generation to the next with their morality tales of cultural values and their accounts of creation.

"Sadly, in our de-mythologized scientific culture, these stories and myths are portrayed as falsehoods. In reality, myths contain profound truths at a depth of meaning where facts are irrelevant. They are stories of adventure and mystery, often of heroic deeds, by imaginary figures that illustrate the deeper truths of life embodied in the spirit. They come as close as words can get to the experience of life itself. We simply don't have the language for it, for the language of life is nonverbal. Which, of course, is why we have the arts. You and I can talk about spirit, but ultimately the power lies in experiencing it."

"Perhaps we have a language for it, but it's not the language of business."

"Language will always be inadequate," acknowledged the Wizard, "but until we accept spirit at least as an equal partner with matter, we will forever undervalue its limitless potential. After all, what are the limits of integrity, will, awareness, initiative, trust, ethics, or compassion? This is the qualitative context of management, indeed of life itself. Its potential power to influence is unlimited."

"Potential power to influence—that's what it's all about, isn't it! Why didn't you say so before?"

"I thought it was apparent." The Wizard smiled at me. "I am pleased you have made the connection. Speaking of connections, you connect with others when you create and channel energy. Others feel its unseen presence which extends beyond the boundaries of our bodies. You influence others with the power of your being, with who you are. You influence them with your qualitative essence, with your spirit, with the magic of what *is*."

"There's that word again!"

"It is pretty basic. Remember, when it is all said and done, is *is*." The Wizard paused to allow that to sink in.

"Is *is*," I muttered to myself.

The Wizard continued, "The point is this: When you strip away all the trappings, the pretenses, the defenses, the hang-ups, the fears, and the rationalizations, you are left with essence; and essence is pure spirit, pure qualitative energy manifested in a being . . . a human *being*. I bet you never thought about that word."

"What word?"

"Being."

"Can't say that I have," I answered with a shrug

"Being comes from the verb *to be*," said the Wizard. "We are human beings, not human *havings* or human *doings*. Hamlet said, 'To be or not to be, that is the question.' He did not say, 'To do or not to do.' Nor did he say, 'To have or not to have.' Being is a higher order than having or doing. William James said, 'Lives based on having or doing are less free than lives based on being.' Life at the being level frees you from the dependence of having and doing. You do not have to do anything. You do not have to have something. You are free to be yourself."

"I'm afraid I don't understand."

"When we talked about the placebo, I said you are free when you are not totally dependent on external things and on other people. You are free when you do not have to *have* something or . . ."

". . . or have to *do* something," I interjected. "The choice is mine at all times."

"There you have it."

"But what has this got to do with being?" I wondered. "I don't get the connection."

Alphie had returned from her hunt and was lying at her master's feet. The Wizard reached down and stroked her. The basset responded by rolling gently over to one side to expose her belly. For a minute or so, the Wizard massaged her, then he looked up at me.

"We love dogs because they *are*."

I waited for the Wizard to complete his thought, but he was not forthcoming. I was accustomed to pauses when talking with him, but being impatient, I picked up on the Wizard's words: "Dogs are what?"

"They just *are*. Nothing more," said the Wizard. "Alphie is pure dog, pure being. In her world, there is no pretense, no deceit, no manipulation, no head-games, no hidden agendas, no guilt-trips, or no hang-ups. She is not trying to live up to her dog-parents' expectations, nor is she trying to persuade us that she is something other than what she is. She just *is*, and we love her for it.

With a twinkle in his eye the Wizard drew closer. "I have this theory that if people were as authentic as dogs, we would not need pets—people would be our pets! I do not mean that we would own our friends and sport them about on leashes, but rather that we would find others so attractive with their naturalness that there would be no need for pets. Now, with so many people trying to impress us, trying to be someone other than themselves, trying to say what is proper or politically correct, trying to tell us what they think we want to hear, we lavish our affection on pets because we can count on their being authentic. Authenticity is an endangered state among humans. If we lived as authentically as dogs, we too would be equally trustworthy and loved for what we are, not for what we do."

"But who would fetch my newspaper?" I asked, playing along with the Wizard's whim.

"Or retrieve your ducks," said the Wizard, continuing to scratch Alphie's belly. "I will concede that there will still be certain specialized functions that pets can perform better than us, but not affection. Seriously, as humans we complicate our lives so. We can learn simplicity from dogs. The key is to start with being."

Playfully, I asked, "Will it help if you scratch my belly, Wizard?"

He laughed and put his arm on my shoulder, pleased with the lighter side in me. "Speaking of scratching, most of us spend a lifetime scratching for a living to acquire the things we should *have* . . . in order that we can then *do* what we want . . . so that we will eventually *be* someone. As a result, we seldom achieve in a lifetime what ought to be our starting point."

"And the starting point is?" I pursued.

"Yes."

"Yes? I asked you about the starting point."

"You said, 'And the starting point *is*,' and I said, 'Yes' because the starting point is with *is*."

"I should have known," I said, contritely. "You *are* the Wizard of Is."

"And *is* is a form of the verb *to be*. *Being* is the starting point. Remember, we are human beings by nature, but we are human havings and human doings by choice. Most of us put having first. We say, 'When I have enough money . . . When I have enough time . . . When I have enough power . . . I will then be able to do what I want and then I will be happy.' In this acquisitive process, we put off being. As a result, we may achieve everything that is external, or *having* success, but we postpone what is internal, or *being* success. In other words, we postpone life in order to make a living. That is a costly tradeoff. True success starts inside with being and works its way out in all that we do.

"You're saying that if I spend my life making a living, then I'm really postponing life itself—what you call inner success. Is that right?"

"Yes, you are deferring the inner life, but if you recall I said life has the two journeys, inner and outer. The full life is a balance of the two. What you are neglecting are the purpose and meaning of life and that makes you very vulnerable."

"Vulnerable?"

"You have, in effect tied your worth to your job. Therefore, as your job goes, so goes your life. In today's dizzying kaleidoscope of change, that is a recipe for disaster. In your effort to create a secure future, you have forged an alliance with insecurity. Building a life on outer success makes you subject to the whims and vagaries of the external world. In biblical terms, it's building your house on sand. Personal security can only come from within. Furthermore, outer success does not prepare you to handle the inevitable crises of life. Only by attending to our being can we cope with the crises and savor fully the richness of life."

"That's what you meant when you said I have to put spirit first?"

"Yes. A human being is intrinsically spiritual. We are pure spirit, encased in a mortal body. When you start with being, you begin with who you are. That is why you take the inner journey to find some answers to life's existential questions: Who am I? Why am I here? What do I value? What are my gifts? What is my purpose in life? Knowing more about yourself, you can then make choices to do or not do, based on what you believe. When you live authentically by putting *being* first, you then have the quality of life you want—a life that is congruent with your innermost values and beliefs. In

Havel's words, this is 'living in the truth.' Anything less than this is living a lie."

"For years I've had it all backwards, haven't I?" I said sadly. "I guess most people do."

The Wizard excused himself briefly and walked into the house. He returned with a well-thumbed volume of Emerson's essays. Opening it to a favorite passage, he said, "Listen to this: 'What you are . . . thunders so that I cannot hear what you say to the contrary.' Emerson is saying that what you are is more powerful than what you say. You feel the 'thunder' of another's being. *Being* is the context that holds the content of your behavior. As an energy force, it surrounds and encompasses all that you say and do. Words and actions have meaning only in the context of being, of who you are. Being must come first."

"This is the same power you felt when you met Mother Teresa, isn't it?"

"Yes, it is very strong with her, despite her age," said the Wizard. "Her being 'thunders so' that it matters little what she says. Being is not only the context for what you say and do, it is also our commonality—the community you have with others."

"Meaning?"

"We all *have* different things, and we all *do* different things, but at the being level, we are one. As human *beings,* we share the same qualities. This is our commonality with all people. When you relate at the being level, all differences of race, gender, and political preference are irrelevant. The trouble starts when you let your differences obscure your common being.

"Jung said, 'Mankind is not just an accumulation of individuals utterly different from one another, but possess such a high degree of psychological collectivity that in comparison the individual appears merely as a slight variant.' This commonality of being is much greater than what sets us apart.

"In a major initiative to end the Cold War, President Kennedy said, 'Let us not be blind to our differences—but let us also direct our attention to our common interests and to the means by which those differences can be resolved.' Common interests are the means to resolve differences."

"Being is the common denominator," I recalled, "that allows me to assimilate the differences of others."

"Your capacity for tolerance grows with your being," affirmed the Wizard. "The ancient Greek oracle at Delphi commanded us to 'Know Thyself.' "

"I was never certain what that meant. It seemed so self-evident."

"Knowing oneself is self-awareness, a capacity unique to humans. Therefore, as you develop this capacity for self-awareness, you will become more fully human. 'Know thyself' means know that you are fully human and live accordingly," explained the Wizard.

"How do I become more self-aware?"

"That's the purpose of the inner journey. It allows us to come to grips with those existential questions and explore the meaning of life. This exploration will reveal the qualities of your being and allow them to show through in everything you do. Tap into your essence, those qualities that resonate with all others. This requires that you reposition the true center of your self from your *head* to your *heart*. Only then you will experience the real power of self-awareness "

"Do you mean to let my emotions take over?" I asked skeptically.

"No, not at all," said the Wizard. "That is a popular misconception. The word *heart,* as I use it, is much more all-encompassing. Emotions are only a piece of it. Heart is an integration or a centeredness of all that you are. Heart is your humanness, your spirit, your authentic being, your *is,* your *how to be.*"

"The real me," I said. "But doesn't the real me include my head and my intellect, too?"

"To be sure. But remember, thoughts are a lower order, a more peripheral dimension of the self."

"All right, so having recentered myself from my head to my heart, what then?"

"Then you can bring your heart, this new center of authentic human power, into everything that you say and do. And you can do it with style and individuality. You may cloak your being with a mantel of words and actions to make it uniquely yours. This is what Jung called *individuation,* the process of becoming a complete individual. It is your heart that stamps all your deeds with your seal of authenticity, because it comes from within. You are then 'living in the truth,' your truth."

"I could feel the intensity of your words," I responded humbly. "That's a pretty convincing demonstration."

"You heard the words," the Wizard corrected, "but you felt the 'thunder' of my being. For you, it was 'heartfelt.' We *do* extend far beyond the physical dimensions of our bodies, you see. The heart is the force you felt. The words are from the head. The heart is what makes you uniquely human, so you need to employ it in all your human affairs. The head is insufficient by itself. Such is the limitation of facts. Life is larger than reason and intellect. With the heart, you are dealing with the whole of what it means to be human. Only the heart can adequately address human concerns."

"Communicating from the heart is *being.* Is that what you're saying?" I wanted to be sure.

"Right," said the Wizard. "That's what gives the heart the power to connect. Being is the container, the context in which you say and do things. When you said you could feel my words, you actually felt the context of my heart which carried those words. To feel them, however, you had to be listening with your heart. We were connecting on a being level. This is called *intimacy.*"

"Intimacy?"

"Yes. Intimacy is heart talk," said the Wizard. "I believe we are all on a quest for intimacy, but most of us do not know how to find it. And when we do, we are often not prepared for it and we do not know what to do with it. Without the inner journey, you feel vulnerable and threatened by intimacy. That is when the ego intervenes with its defenses to rescue you from intimacy. The ego does not know that it is rejecting the essence of life. You need to start with *being* and that will determine your choices for *doing*."

"You're telling me that I get too caught up in doing things without attending to the spirit of what I'm doing. What counts is the spirit, the quality of being, that I bring to the act of doing. Rather than concentrate on doing, I need to focus on being. Then I can bring those qualities of being into everything I do. *Being* stamps uniqueness on all I do. Is that right?"

"You said it well," affirmed the Wizard. "The world is full of human *havings* and human *doings,* but it is rather short on human *beings*."

My face lit up. "I love it—human havings and human doings! They certainly rule in numbers."

"Ah, but human beings rule in quality," rejoined the Wizard. "Being is the source of quality because quality begins with human qualities, with the human spirit. When we put spirit first, others experience that spirit and feel energized. This is the human connection. Experiencing another person's spirit is like breathing fresh air. Like any essence, its power lies in its purity. The more pure the exposure, the greater the impact. Pure love. Pure joy. These are the qualities that carry the messages. People put too much faith in words. We think our words will be influential. But words without the infusion of spirit are devoid of life, impotent. Conviction, commitment, sincerity, trust, joy, sensitivity—these are the qualities that give our words and deeds the power to influence. This is the same energy that extends beyond our bodies and creates 'action at a distance.' This is what sells—the invisible qualities of being, of what *is*."

"Once again, I can feel the power of your words . . . rather, of your being," I said, not knowing quite what I felt.

"When a person you love or respect says something, it has more impact than the same words spoken by someone you do not love or respect. Love and respect are powers of the heart. In a less influential context, the words would have no power," asserted the Wizard.

Translating this into my business world, I replied, "Being

'sells.' Being adds value. It brings a quality of authenticity to any business transaction."

"Let me tell you a story," said the Wizard. "Recently I talked with a Fortune 500 manager who could 'see' his division becoming the most respected in his industry. This was his personal vision. To him, respect was a quality that fired him with energy and zeal. Respect was the spirit, the qualitative context within which he did business. When he shared his personal vision with his senior manager, the latter, unaware of his feelings about respect, asked him to change the word 'respected' to 'profitable.' He strongly resisted, but eventually he agreed to add 'profitable' without deleting 'respected.'

"He told me later that he was not going to let his manager remove the word from his vision. He spoke with such feeling, it was apparent that this was the source of this man's energy. Removing respect from his vision statement would have taken the vitality and purpose out of it. Generating profits did not arouse his passion. Generating respect did.

"The roots of this manager's feelings went back over a quarter of a century and tapped into the very essence of the man. His actions were flowing from the core of his being, from his heart. For him, material profits will follow when the heart is activated. To know this man was to know that respect was the source of his energy. Wise leaders know how to tap into this energy and release its power. Regrettably, this man's manager did not."

"The man in your story acted with great personal integrity."

"You have used a powerful word," said the Wizard. "*Integrity* comes from a Latin word meaning 'untouched,' hence 'undivided' or 'whole.' When we act with integrity, we act as an undivided whole. This is what gives integrity its laser-like power. It is not fragmented nor is it fractured. It comes 'untouched' from the core of our being. We admire people who show integrity because they are being true to their inner selves. This is what Vaclav Havel meant by living openly in the 'sphere of truth.' Havel's real power lies not in his words, where he shows great mastery as a playwright, but in his integrity. This is the quality that people admire. As a leader, he thunders with integrity. He is what he says.

"In his address to the U. S. Congress, Havel said, 'The salvation of this human world lies nowhere else than in the human heart, in the human power to reflect, in human meekness, and in human responsibility.' Tell me, does this not say *how to be?*"

"He certainly says what you've been saying."

"Saying it is one thing, but taking initiative and acting on it is quite another. That is where Havel excels, and that is everyone's responsibility," said the Wizard. "It is your responsibility and it is mine. That is the way life is."

Suggestions

- Are you more of a human having or a human doing rather than a human being? Take some time to assess your qualities and those of your business staff. Begin with yourself:

  1. What are my salient qualities ? You may wish to ask others for opinions.
  2. Which of these qualities do I feel passionate about? (What inspires me?)
  3. Do others feel this energy of mine at work?
  4. What can I do to reveal more of "who I am"? How can I let what is truly me show through? (How can I let the *is* shine?)

- Give the same four questions to each of your staff members. Ask them to assess themselves and prepare to discuss their findings with you.

Now ask yourself the same four questions about each of your key staff people:

  1. What are his/her salient qualities?
  2. Which of these qualities does he/she feel passionate about?

3. Does this energy come through in his/her relationships at work? If so, how does it show? If not, why not?
4. What can he/she do to reveal more of who they are?

- Share and discuss what you have observed with each staff person. Compare and contrast your observations about each of them with their thoughts about themselves. Tell each person what you are trying to do for yourself and ask for their help. Also ask what you can do, or not do, to help them reveal more of "who they are" at work. Then you can agree to take specific action steps to release more of this how-to-be energy.

15
The Pull and Push of Life

If you wish to change another person's behavior,
the surest way is to change your own behavior.

The story of the manager who wanted to make his division "the most respected" had sunk deeply into my consciousness. I wondered how often I had been guilty of imposing my ways upon my staff, and I pondered the effect this had on their productivity and happiness. I discovered that when I thought about people qualitatively, I started to behave differently toward them. I was eager to talk with each of them to determine what qualities they valued and to see if they were flourishing in the work setting. Then, I thought about what turned me on in life, and I concluded it was helping people develop to their fullest potential. I enjoyed the sense of achievement that came from helping others.

I tried to summarize what I had learned: "My essence is spirit. Spirit manifests itself in my being—in my heart or true self. My being is the destination of the inner journey of self-awareness when I follow the command to 'Know Thyself.' *Being* is the context of all that I say and do. When I begin with being, I bring these qualities of the heart into all my choices. If I can bring being to the forefront of my life, then I will live a life governed by inner truths that emerge from the heart, not one dictated by external circumstances. What one *is* influences what one *does*. This is a life of integrity."

It was very satisfying for me to understand what the Wizard had said, and to summarize it in my own words. I felt I had come a long way, but one thing still troubled me. It had concerned me since I first heard the Wizard discuss humility—it all sounded too passive. After all, I was a person used to taking action, and it was not enough for me to be open to influence by others. I also needed to influence others actively. The Wizard touched on this with the power of being and integrity, but I wanted to hear more.

When we met again, the Wizard had a large map spread out on the table. He told me he was going to take a trip to the high country of Baltistan, a region of Kashmir in northern Pakistan. It is a spectacularly beautiful land, and the only area in the world where three of the world's highest mountain ranges come together—the Himalayas, the Karakorams, and the Hindu Kush. When I asked him what he intended to do there, the Wizard said that he enjoyed trekking in the more remote regions. He drew inspiration from these treks. The physical demands and the majestic solitude of these locations seemed to give him a new balance, a recentering of his being. To my amazement, the Wizard told me that he would be gone for a long time.

"I am going to miss our meetings," I told him. "They have become a very important part of my life."

The Wizard smiled and, taking the compliment graciously, modestly replied, "We are an addictive society, and I think we can get addicted to anything. It is not good to be too dependent. If I were doing my job properly, you would not feel the need to continue. The 'doctor within' would feel sufficiently confident to begin its own practice."

"I think the doctor isn't through medical school yet!" I chuckled. "Perhaps it just needs a year in residency."

"Life is all the residency it needs. Your doctor will do very well. Believe me," insisted the Wizard, "it just takes practice."

"Thank you for your confidence. I needed that placebo. But when do you expect to return?"

"I do not really know. I may not," said the Wizard. "I never put a return time on these trips because I never know what will come of them. When the time comes, I will know what to do."

I was stunned. The Wizard had never indicated before that he was thinking of leaving. "You mean you may not come back to the United States?"

For the first time, I felt a slight distance in the Wizard's manner as he spoke. "There is always that possibility. You have your calling and I have mine, and we each must respond to our own inner voice. I came here because I felt called to do so. My intuition tells me that I will probably be called elsewhere. But that I cannot say. I will know only when it happens."

"But what about the practice you've established, and all the friends you've made?" I asked. "And then there's the children."

"They will always be with me," said the Wizard. "As Americans, we tend to be very generous and hospitable people. Many people around the world are very fond of us and our open ways, but we tend to think that America is the only place to live. There are lovely people elsewhere, and we would be well advised to get to know them and their customs. We have much to learn from others. Because English is the universal language, others must make the effort to learn it. This can lead to arrogance and stultifying complacency for us. We must reach out. The world needs us and we need others as well. We are all interconnected. Reaching out is a responsibility that requires initiative and patience, trust and forgiveness, compassion and discipline. It is not an easy role, but it is vital and potentially very rewarding."

"Your words are well-chosen, Wizard. Thanks for your caring advice."

"You are welcome," said the Wizard. "You have used one of my favorite words: care. You need to practice intensive care. Not the high-tech, hospital stuff, but what John Naisbitt calls the 'high-touch,' human stuff."

"High-touch," I repeated. "That says it, doesn't it?"

"Yes, but it is not enough to say it," asserted the Wizard. "You must *feel* it. Intensive care comes from the heart. It has healing power. You know its presence when you feel it. When you care, any relationship is very forgiving. Actions are less important in the context of care. For example, people do not know what to say when a friend has a life-threatening ill-ness—take your cancer, for example. In truth, it matters little what people say to you. What is important is that you know that the other person cares. A woman who lived for months with her young, dying daughter told me she learned the power of simply 'being there with love.' That is intimacy."

"That's very touching." My manner softened as I spoke. "You didn't mention the placebo, but I see it working its won-drous ways through the mother's care."

"You are absolutely right. I simply forgot to make that con-nection. Will you forgive me?" The Wizard smiled, knowing it was done.

"You don't even have to ask. In the context of care, for-giveness is easy."

The Wizard, allowing himself a pinch of pride, put his arm around me. "You do not need me any more. The answers that lie within seem to be emerging. You have come a long way in the times we have been together."

"Thank you." I was feeling a sense of inner composure, largely unknown to me months before. "I feel much better about myself, and it shows in my relationships. That's the test.

"There is one more thing you could help me with, however. You have been a role model for me, as I have tried to be for my business associates. Many of them are action types who might see this whole *how-to-be* process as too passive. I'm afraid my influence on them will not have the impact yours has had on me."

"I thought you might feel that way," said the Wizard. "That is why I closed our last session with those few words on ini-tiative. You may recall that I said it all starts within us. The whole process is dynamic and ever-changing. If I have con-veyed the image of passivity, I have not been very effective."

"Perhaps I was too sweeping in my generalization," I said. "I specifically mean the emphasis on opening yourself to another's influence. How do I actively influence someone else?"

"I feel your concern," said the Wizard. "There are several factors here. First, you must remember that you cannot control others, only yourself. You cannot insure the openness of others, but you can insure your own openness. If you are open and non-defensive, you increase the chance that others will be, too. With no need to defend yourself, your energy can then be directed toward relating to others, rather than protecting yourself."

"You're saying there is power to influence others in just being open and non-defensive?"

"Spot on!" affirmed the Wizard. "You must not underestimate the power of openness. When you open yourself to another, you are giving, and giving can break through the toughest resistance. It is one of those paradoxes—in receiving another, you give of yourself. This is a placebo. It says we care."

"Actually, what I thought was a passive act is really a powerful placebo."

"Being receptively open is vital, but you must also be expressively open." The Wizard's face came alive as he spoke. "If you wish to change another person's behavior, the surest way is to change your own behavior. This means doing new and different things. You are forever trying to change another without the inconvenience of having to change yourself. Changing your behavior will induce an altered response from the other person. I think this is one of the least understood truisms of management.

"When you have ideas you believe to be right and good, you should advocate them passionately. In doing so, however, you must not be closed to others. If you recall, my objection is with fixed opinions, not opinions per se. In a relationship, the creative process demands that you merge your feelings as well as your ideas with the other person's feelings and thoughts—literally absorbing each other at the being level. In effect, the two of you become one for the moment.

"It is this creative interfusion that gives rise to new possibilities that neither of us could have imagined. I said this process was risky because you had to let go of your desire for a certain outcome. By definition, the outcome of any creative endeavor is unknown. This is also true in human interaction. You must trust the process. This is a time for simply allowing, a consciously induced 'come what may.' In effect, it is a moment of surrender to the creative process."

"Wizard, that's not an easy thing to do when we think we have all the answers. That's the ego, I guess. Generally speaking, I don't like to surrender anything to anybody."

"And that is why creativity is such a rare and highly prized quality," said the Wizard. "It is also why people have such an absence of meaningful communication at a feeling level. Ideas lead to conflict; feelings lead to commonality."

"What do you mean by that?"

"Our human condition is what we have in common," said the Wizard. "We differ in our customs, our beliefs, and our ideologies. *Communication* comes from a Latin word meaning 'common.' Communication is commonality. Although we may disagree in our beliefs, we can find commonality in matters of the heart. We are all moved by compassion, inspired by truth, touched by care, heartened by hope, stirred by love, and emboldened by courage. This is the commonality of being, the irreducible *is*."

"This is what you meant when you said that spirit influences. These are the timeless qualities that endure, the essence that you spoke of. They speak to our common humanity, to what *is*." I suddenly sounded very much like the Wizard.

"There you are. You activated the wizard within you! Essence *is*," said the Wizard, holding up his forefinger.

"The 'wizard within.' I like that. It has alliterative power. Is that like the 'doctor within'?"

"No difference. The doctor is the wizard; the wizard the doctor. Now let us focus on your concern for action. You recall, the visualization process is linked to action. Mental imagery is an action step. We also talked about the 'cognitive receptivity' that comes with a relaxed awareness, and how you could reprogram yourself with positive images, emotions, actions, and affirmations. This is a consciously directed effort of choice.

"*Passive* implies an absence of active choice. In any situation, never say, 'I had no choice.' You always have a choice. The process starts with the 'pull' of awareness."

"The pull of awareness?"

"Exactly," said the Wizard. "The pull of awareness is mindfulness, your capacity to absorb everything around you—people, ideas, feelings, ambiance. You recall our discussion on centering and concentration. That process heightens your awareness and develops the 'doctor within.' This doctor makes its practice available to you. It is only this openness to all things and all people that enables you to see the multiplicity of possibilities that arise from the interconnectedness of people and events. The more connections you experience, the more options you have for action. When you look at a situation too narrowly, you diminish your chances to change it."

"Change it! That's what I mean. I have to take action to shape events and make changes. I can't just passively wait for people and events to come my way."

"You are advocating the other half of this dynamic process, the 'push' of *initiative*." Thrusting his arm forward, the Wizard continued. "The process demands that you reach out. The push of initiative involves taking risks by getting out of your 'comfort zones,' breaking habit patterns, seeking possibilities, trying new things, being curious, exploring new facets of life, becoming adventurous, making and admitting mistakes, asking and giving forgiveness, meeting new people, changing routines, experimenting—all of these and more. Above all, it means taking initiative and being accountable for the consequences. This is an energizing process. It is aliveness."

"I can feel your aliveness," I said admiringly.

"You are experiencing what we are talking about. There is a rhythm and flow to life and its events. The creative process is all about being aware of this and knowing when and how to intervene actively to shape and direct the energy. Having sensed the possibilities that exist in a situation, you may move on any of them. *Action* naturally follows *awareness*. This is the pull and push of life. It is a natural dialogue of action, not the forced action of demands and compliance that is so unproductive. Now, does this sound too passive for you?"

"Not at all."

"Life is a mix of action and reflection, the latter being the more passive. Too much of either, however, is a life out of balance. While reflection has nothing to show for itself without action, action without reflection has little meaning or purpose. The old adage, 'The unexamined life is not worth living,' attests to the power of reflection. You need both to be complete," concluded the Wizard.

"In a broader sense, you're really talking about negotiation, aren't you?"

"Yes, but what I described runs deeper than traditional negotiation theory would care to admit."

"Everything you talk about runs deeper."

"That is the untold story, isn't it?" said the Wizard. "If you acknowledge the power of the implicit, you have to go deeper to get behind the explicit. You have to get closer to the source. That is the inner journey. That is *how to be*. To do so takes you closer to what *is*."

"It sounds as if we're back to where we started—back to what *is*."

"Did we ever leave?"

"I guess not, but you said 'closer to what *is*.' Do you think I'll ever really get there?"

"Everything hinges on awareness," maintained the Wizard. "The source of life has always been there for you to discover. In that sense, it is always available to you. In another sense, you can never hope to know fully what *is*. The 'part' cannot grasp the nature of the greater whole. In a spiritual sense, creatures can never fully fathom the nature of their Creator. A lesser power is incapable of fully comprehending the greater power.

"So perhaps you shall never know what really *is*. That is the role of faith, hope, and trust. But you can cleanse your perceptions. In doing so, you will operate closer to the limits of your powers. You do not know those limits yet and so you must forever test and challenge them. That is what makes life such an adventure. And that, my dear friend, is the way life is."

Suggestions

The Wizard teaches balance. A "how-to-be life" is a balance between the pull of awareness and the push of initiative. Awareness is a receptive, more reflective skill. Initiative is an expressive, more action-focused skill. Most people are deficient in one or both of these dimensions. Our culture emphasizes action with its "Do something!" mentality. We pay little attention to awareness, yet this may be the most important skill any of us will ever learn. The key to awareness is being mindful. Many of us are so stressed-out that we lose both our mindfulness and the will to initiate. The following suggestions are designed to help you develop both awareness and initiative:

To Help You Strengthen the Pull of Awareness:

- Take a mindful walk, preferably barefoot. Walk in a very slow pace being mindful of the body's action in lifting your legs and placing them down again. Listen to the sounds and feel the sensations on your feet. Think of this walk as a very slow moving meditation with full concentration on your movement.
- Eat a raisin (or a nut) mindfully. Jon Kabat-Zinn, director of the Stress Reduction Clinic at the University of Massachusetts, uses this as his first meditation exercise. Look at the raisin, feel it, smell it, and taste it very slowly. Note the action of the salivary glands before you put it in your mouth. The idea here is to be mindful of something we normally do without thinking.
- Scan your body mindfully. Sit, as in the relaxation response, or lie on a soft, firm surface with arms at your side, feet slightly apart, and a support under your head.

Starting with your feet, focus your attention on a muscle group and release any tension in it as you breathe out. Pretend that all your stress and tension is being expelled with each breath. Move through your body taking as much time as you wish. When you finish, you will be in a more relaxed and mindful state.

- The relaxation response, where we focused on our breathing (in chapter 8), is a mindful exercise.
- Create your own mindful exercises.

Mindfulness increases as you and I take a fresh approach to life. Ellen Langer's research at Harvard taught her that change requires two things: learning to think about old situations in new ways, and opening up and enlarging your frame of reference.

To help you strengthen the Push of Initiative:

- Before you begin a new initiative, do a mindful exercise like one of those above. Then look for new ways to approach your situation. Reframe the situation in a larger context, like a broader scope or a longer time span. This will increase your options just as a narrow perspective limits them.
- Risk is usually associated with loss. Reframe your risk-taking in terms of gain. Visualize those gains, then act as if they were so.
- Learn to live with "creative uncertainty." Don't attach yourself to any necessary outcome. Strive to make things happen, but if they don't, accept the new outcome and move on.
- Take a look at your habit patterns. Are you too comfortable? Have you lost your edge? If so, jar yourself out of the mindset with an adventurous curiosity that seeks different ways.
- Be a possibility seeker first. Then be a problem solver in the context of this new potential.
- Reinvent yourself periodically as artists do evolving

through different periods in their lives. Your life is your art form.

- Forgive yourself and others of all mistakes and move on. Don't wallow in regret, remorse, or recrimination.
- Take action, and be mindful of your heightened awareness and your aliveness.

Epilogue

To be or not to be: that is the question.
—*William Shakespeare*

The Wizard and I departed with embraces and great affection. He never did return to the United States, and nobody knows for certain where he went. Rumors, of course, abound. Some say he got caught in the Kashmir border conflict between India and Pakistan. Others say he is working in the devastated villages of Afghanistan. Still others believe he lives as a guru somewhere in the remote regions of neighboring China. He remains, as before, a mystery.

Curious things have happened, however. I am still coping with cancer, but my health has gained new vigor as all aspects of my life shine with being. And to my dismay, I have become somewhat of a folk hero myself! People come to talk with me about how I achieved my success. One reporter labeled me "The Wizard of the Workplace." I am uncomfortable with that sobriquet, because I claim no special talents. But I do say I was fortunate to learn some things from a man who taught me to consult the "doctor within."

When asked by a reporter what I had learned from this man, I replied, "In an age where everything seems to be relative, there are some enduring qualities of the human spirit. These qualities are our common humanity. They are the special qualities of being, of human being. Like the mountain massifs of Kashmir, they simply are. The inner journey is a quest for this source of our being, this wellspring of our humanness. It provides a rich and inexhaustible supply of energy that permeates all we have and do. It is the context of all our relationships, and it possesses enormous power to influence and to heal. It is the implicit state that surrounds all management and leadership principles, practices, and policies. It is the essence of life, the truth of human affairs, the irreducible *is*. If I have enjoyed any degree of success, it has been because I have attended to this."

With that, I said, "That is the way life is," and set out with the reporter for a brisk walk around the workplace.

Bibliography

Adams, John D., Ph.D., General Editor. *Transforming Work.* Miles River, 1984.

_____. *Transforming Leadership.* Miles River, 1986.

Assagioli, Roberto, M.D. *The Act of Will.* Penguin, 1974.

Benson, Herbert, M.D. *Your Maximum Mind.* Times Books, 1987.

Blanchard, Kenneth, Ph.D. and Spencer Johnson, M.D. *The One Minute Manager.* William Morrow & Co., 1981.

Campbell, Joseph with Bill Moyers. *The Power of Myth.* Doubleday, 1988.

Chopra, Deepak, M.D. *Quantum Healing: Exploring the Frontiers of Mind/Body Medicine.* Bantam Books, 1989.

Cousins, Norman. *Anatomy of an Illness.* W. W. Norton, 1979.

_____. *Head First: The Biology of Hope.* E. P. Dutton, 1989.

Csikszentmihalyi, *Mihaly. Flow: The Psychology of Optimal Experience.* Harper Perennial, 1990.

Dossey, Larry, M.D. *Meaning and Medicine: A Doctor's Tales of Breakthrough and Healing.* Bantam Books, 1991.

Gallwey, Timothy W. *The Inner Game of Tennis*. Bantam Books, 1984.

Gallwey, Timothy W. and Bob Kriegel. *The Inner Game of Skiing*. Pan Books, 1987.

Hammerschlag, Carl A., M.D. *The Theft of the Spirit: A Journey to Spiritual Healing with Native Americans*. Simon & Schuster, 1993.

Havel, Vaclav. *Living in Truth*. Faber and Faber., 1987.

Hawley, Jack. *Reawakening the Spirit in Work: The Power of Dharmic Management*. Berrett-Koehler, 1993.

Kabat-Zinn, Jon. *Wherever You Go, There You Are*. Hyperion, 1994.

Kornfield, Jack. *A Path with Heart: A Guide through the Perils and Promises of Spiritual Life*. Bantam Books, 1993.

Jung, Carl G. *Psychological Reflections*. Princeton University Press, 1970.

Langer, Ellen J. *Mindfulness*. Addison-Wesley, 1989.

Leider, Richard J. *Life Skills: Taking Charge of Your Personal and Professional Growth*. Pfeiffer, 1993.

_____. *Repacking Your Bags: Lighten Your Load for the Rest of Your Life*. Berrett-Koehler, 1995.

Levine, Stephen. *A Gradual Awakening*. Anchor Books/ Doubleday, 1989.

Meyers, Casey. *Walking: A Complete Guide to the Complete Exercise*. Random House, 1992.

Moyers, Bill. *Healing and the Mind*. Doubleday, 1993.

Owen, Harrison. *Riding the Tiger: Doing Business in a Transforming World*. Abbott Publishing, 1991.

_____. *Leadership Is*. Abbott Publishing, 1990.

_____. *Spirit: Transformation and Development in Organizations*. Abbott Publishing, 1987.

Padus, Emrika (*Prevention* Editors) *The Complete Guide to Your Emotions and Your Health: New Dimensions in Mind/Body Healing*. Rodale Press, 1986.

Pelletier, Kenneth R. *Mind as Healer, Mind as Slayer: A Holistic Approach to Preventing Stress Disorders*. Delta, 1977.

_____. *Sound Mind, Sound Body: A New Model for Lifelong Health*. Simon & Schuster, 1994.

Schumacher, E. F. *Small Is Beautiful*. Harper and Row, 1973.

_____. *A Guide for the Perplexed*. Harper and Row, 1977.

Selye, Hans, M.D. *Stress without Distress*. Signet, 1974.

Shealy, C. Norman, M.D., Ph.D. and Caroline M. Myss. *The Creation of Health: The Emotional, Psychological, and Spiritual Responses that Promote Healing*. Stillpoint Publishing, 1993.

Sheldrake, Rupert. *The Presence of the Past: Morphic Resonance and the Habits of Nature*. Collins, 1988.

Siegel, Bernie S. *Love, Medicine and Miracles*. Harper and Row, 1986.

_____. *Peace, Love and Healing*. Harper and Row, 1989.

Sweet, Leonard I. *Quantum Spirituality: A Postmodern Apologetic*. Whaleprints, 1991.

Swimme, Brian. *The Universe Is a Green Dragon: A Cosmic Creation Story*. Bear & Co., 1984.

Weil, Andrew, M.D. *Natural Health, Natural Medicine: A Comprehensive Manual for Wellness and Self-Care*. Houghton Mifflin Company, 1990.

Zukav, Gary. *The Dancing Wu Li Masters: An Overview of the New Physics*. Bantam Books, 1979.

*If the Wizard's words touch you in a way that you'd
like to share with the author, or if you'd like to contact him,
you may write to:*

Tom Thiss
P.O. Box 154
Excelsior, MN 55331